MW01120140

ONCE UPON A PRAYER

Or
Living 'tween two
Denominations

Susan Daniels Poulos

ONCE UPON A PRAYER

Or
Living 'tween two Denominations

Susan Daniels Poulos

Copyright © 2003
All Rights Reserved

No part of this book may be reproduced in any form without written permission from the publishers, except by a reviewer who may quote brief passages in a review to be printed in a newspaper or magazine.

First printing.

All scripture quotations, unless otherwise indicated, are taken from THE HOLY BIBLE, Revised Standard Version.

PUBLISHED BY:
BRENTWOOD CHRISTIAN PRESS
4000 BEALLWOOD AVENUE
COLUMBUS, GEORGIA 31904

Dedication

This book is dedicated to my wonderful husband, John Poulos,
and in the loving memory of my parents,
Myrt and Howard Daniels.

Contents

My Story

Devotional Readings

MY STORY

Introduction

All too often the stories and events that reflect the existence and workings of God in our lives are not told. They are not shared with others. The result--faith in God does not increase nor is God given the glory He deserves.

It is for this reason that this book has been written. The book, titled, "Once Upon a Prayer" subtitled "Living 'tween two Denominations" has been written because the existence and workings of God in my husband John's and my life has, we think, been pretty evident. And as we share with others what the Lord has done in our lives, faith in God, hopefully, will increase, albeit even if it's just "a little bit" as each reader reads this book.

The book has also been written in an effort to point out that God is our creator and finisher. He knows us better than we can ever know ourselves. He knows our strengths and our weaknesses. He knows our gifts and our talents. He knows our successes and our failures. He knows everything, indeed, ALL about us…and, in spite of everything, He loves us with an unconditional and unfailing love, a love that passes all understanding.

To God be the Glory!

Chapter One

Behold, I am Doing a New Thing

"Remember not the former things nor consider the things of old. Behold, I am doing a new thing." (Isaiah 43:18-19)

Having lived 30 years without Jesus in my life, I'd managed to complete college, teach junior high school for seven years, suffer through the devastating unexpected death of my father, get married and subsequently, divorced, and, in general, live a fairly normal life. Like most lives, mine had been filled with a variety of events and milestones. But now I'd begun dating again and the hurts and disillusions of my failed marriage had begun to fade. Mike and I had been going together three and a half years. It looked like our interests and similarities outweighed the differences and perhaps our futures would become intertwined. Marriage was a possibility.

Into this relationship stepped "ole weird Harold," Mike's boss at work. (Actually, we called him that because he was "religious".) 'Ole weird Harold told Mike about a dynamic guest speaker his church was sponsoring for a series of evening meetings. After several promptings to attend one of these evening meetings, we agreed to hear this man. We had nothing else to do, why not?

Sporting a blond Afro-haircut and possessing a dynamic gift for effective speaking, ("ole weird Harold" was right)...this speaker was unlike anyone I'd ever heard before. And at the end of his message he had people jumping to their feet to confess and repent of their sins. Cigarette packages flew onto the stage from every direction as people agreed to give up smoking and follow Jesus. He said, "All you smokers out there...oh, you can go to heaven if you smoke, but you're going to go in smelling a little stinky, now, do you want to meet Jesus THAT way?" And, so he gave an altar call and asked people to confess and repent of their sins or wrongdoings. He told them to walk forward, publicly, to the front of the Sanctuary and ask Jesus Christ into their lives as their Lord and Savior.

Simultaneously and unrehearsed or talked about beforehand, Mike and I stood up and went forward. And, in the front of that Sanctuary we joined the others who asked Christ into their lives that night. We became born–again Christians!

That week, like young children, Mike and I each purchased copies of Hurlbut's "Story of the Bible", (the Bible in storybook form) and we "plowed through it with zeal and determination." Clearly, we thirsted to know better this newfound Lord and Master of our lives!

About that time, something called the "Charismatic Renewal" was sweeping through the United States and before long Mike and I were involved. Gatherings of people, alive for Jesus and filled with the Holy Spirit, were filling church sanctuaries, school gymnasiums, and the Minneapolis Auditorium. It was often "standing room only" as people packed out these places! After hours of praying and praising the Lord with hymns, songs and uplifted hands, no one wanted to go home! Miracles ensued! Clearly, it was an exciting time to be a new born-again Christian!

I began to spend time, each night, in intense prayer, beseeching the Lord to infill me with more of Himself. I wanted to hear His voice and do His will! I cried out, "Help me to lay my life on Your altar, Lord! Help me to go all the way with you, Lord! Guide and direct my life, Lord! Take over!"

Each night's time with the Lord became longer and more intense. The relationship deepened and sometimes, during the course of the day, I could hardly wait until it was time to be with Him. Then, one night I felt prompted to pray, in earnest, for what was at that time in the Charismatic Renewal called, "the Baptism in the Holy Spirit". I wanted to receive that "special infilling, anointing or empowering of the Holy Spirit". I'd seen evidence of people within the Renewal who'd received this added "power from on high" and they were "just different". They had something that other Christians, who didn't have this power, didn't have. There was a "night and day difference." Christians with this added power exhibited the manifestations or gifts of the Holy Spirit. Their gifts differed in that one person might prophecy, another might lay hands on someone and that person would be healed, another might speak in tongues, while another might interpret those tongues. There were various gifts, but whatever gift they were given…empowered Christians were "just different."

Well, I wanted this empowerment, too. If Jesus wanted His people to be "different" I wanted to be that way too. I said "all the way, Jesus," and I meant it! And, so I asked Jesus to baptize me…to send down the Holy Spirit, in a powerful way, into me! Soon, a powerful "flood of warmth came through me and a bright light flashed inside my head." I knew, without a shadow of a doubt, that my prayer had been answered.

In the days that followed, the evidence of the Holy Spirit's presence became clear to me. Among other things, it was absolutely impossible to think negative or bad thoughts about anyone. There was no desire, whatsoever, to judge others, talk about or find fault with them. I was filled with an incredible love for people. It was amazing! I believe that I experienced "just a taste" of the infinite and complete love God has for us! Oh, what love He has for us! Also, as I read my Bible, suddenly scripture verses literally jumped out at me with new found clarity and meaning. It was as if I'd never read the Bible before, such was the clarity and meaning!

Scripture says: "And he (Jesus) went about all of Galilee, teaching in their synagogues and preaching the gospel of the kingdom and healing every disease and every infirmity among the people. And his fame spread throughout all Syria, and they brought Him all the sick, those affiliated with various diseases and pains, demoniacs, epileptics, and paralytics, and He healed them." (Matthew 4:23-24)

Meanwhile, I was still dating Mike and as the Fall hay fever season approached, Mike dreaded it. For over 40 years he'd suffered through hay fever season with red, watery eyes and a red, drippy nose. Often he got headaches to make matters worse. I said, "Mike, let's just pray against your hay fever and get rid of it." The Bible said Jesus could heal our diseases and so I believed it! All we had to do was ask Him! I had a simple child-like faith, but I believed it was just that simple! Ask Jesus and He will do it! And so, I laid my hands on Mike and together we prayed for him to be healed of his hay fever. We'd heard about "binding and casting out in the Name of Jesus", and so we did that too. We bound and cast out the spirit of hay fever. We claimed healing in the Name of Jesus. We believed he was healed. Well, nothing seemed to happen and we were a little disappointed. But, when that year's Fall hay fever season rolled around and was reported to be the worst in years, Mike had absolutely no evidence of it! He'd been healed!

Scripture says: "And whatever you ask in prayer, you will receive, if you have faith." (Matthew 20:22)

Chapter Two

I Will Grant You Your Heart's Desire

"May he grant you your heart's desire, and fulfill all your plans! May we shout for joy over your victory, and in the name of our God set up our banners! May the Lord fulfill all your petitions! Now I know that the Lord will help his anointed; he will answer him from his holy heaven with mighty victories by his right hand."
(Psalms 20:4-6)

After teaching school for seven years, I'd had it and decided not to renew my teaching contract for the next year. I'd sent out countless job resumés and prayed about what the Lord wanted me to do. I had no idea. Mom and I had decided to sell the house and move into an apartment. We'd packed up everything and the house was empty as the moving van pulled away with the last of our belongings. We were about to leave, ourselves, when the phone rang. It was the representative from a check printing company at which I'd interviewed and he offered me a job as a technical writer within the audio-visual department.

Two more minutes and I'd have been gone from the house with no opportunity to accept this phone call. The job might have gone to someone else. I marveled at the perfect timing and then remembered that the Lord's timing is always perfect! All good things work together for those who love the Lord. He will never let us down! His timing and His ways are perfect. And, so I soon began a new job.

Each night as I spent time with the Lord in prayer, I began to pray for my new co-workers, that the Lord would watch over them. There was one single, bachelor fellow I always seemed to pray for last. His name was John Poulos and it wasn't very long before my thoughts were drifting to him more and more, even during the course of the day.

I began to talk with the Lord about John, asking Him if John might, indeed, be His chosen one for me to marry. Over a period of time confirmation of this became pretty evident as one incident after another occurred. First of all, when John planned a vacation trip to San Diego, combining a "look-see" of the company's printing plant along with checking out the housing market it was clear John was considering a job transfer to San Diego. I teased John that he probably wouldn't like it in San Diego this time. That, in fact, the ideal weather that was drawing him to California might not be a reality this time. I kidded him that it might rain on his vacation trip. Nevertheless, he seemed determined and I became nervous and concerned. If he moved there I would never see him again. He'd be out of my life. Suddenly, as I sat at my work desk two words came into my head. "Don't worry". That's exactly what I heard. Just two words...don't worry!

Scripture says: "the Lord searches all hearts, and understands every plan and thought." (I Chron. 28:9)

And, when John returned from his vacation trip to San Diego he tossed the newspaper on my work desk. I was flabbergasted to read the headlines: "Rain Continues". It had rained almost the whole time he'd been on vacation! Oh, naturally, I felt a little guilty, but at the same time I couldn't help smiling. Clearly, a greater power than me was in charge here!

Mike and I broke up and I began dating John in March, 1974. We said the marriage vows and got married in September, but not before we'd "put it to the Lord". He'd confirmed that He approved of this marriage, but I even wanted Him to "set the date". I was dead serious that I wanted to do what was right according to His will. I consulted Him about everything. John and I were head-over-heals in love and quite anxious to get married, but we "held out" until the fifth of September and then we were married in John's church, St. Mary's Greek Orthodox Church, in Minneapolis, Minnesota.

It was a very small, private wedding with only the best man and his wife, my Mom, John's Mom, his Sister, and the priest's wife, there. (In the Orthodox church priests can marry if they do so before ordination.)

Fear gripped me as the wedding ceremony proceeded. I was a Charismatic Protestant woman marrying a Greek Orthodox man in his church and everything about the ceremony was strange and unfamiliar to me. What had I gotten myself into? Had I made another terrible mistake?

I knew enough about the Orthodox church to know that it was very liturgical in its Sunday services. There were very few differences from one Sunday service to the next and that was quite different from what I was used to in the Charismatic Lutheran churches I'd been attending. Clearly, the two churches were at opposite ends of the Christian spectrum. One was very staid and formal, the other quite flexible and informal.

I listened closely as the priest performed the ceremony, refer-ring to me as the "handmaid of the Lord, joined together with John, as the servant of the Lord." Was this a wise thing I was doing, marrying this man? Would a marriage between two people from such opposite Christian denominations survive?

We were married on a Friday evening, but on Saturday I was to begin realizing that I'd married a genuinely wonderful person when John accompanied me to my church. We didn't rush off on a honeymoon. No, not at all. We had something far more impor-tant to do. We recognized that we had one serious problem area and it needed to be addressed. We couldn't ignore it! So, we went to my church, East Immanuel Lutheran Church, in St. Paul, and alone, in the quiet darkness of the Sanctuary, we knelt at the altar rail and asked Jesus Christ to be the "Lord of our Marriage". We asked Him to be at the CENTER of our marriage. We'd done that through the marriage vows at John's church the day before and now we did it at my church the day afterwards. Double asking, double coverage! We did this because we knew that otherwise our marriage would never survive. It would end in failure unless He was at the center...between us! Why, you might ask? Well, ironically enough, if there was anything that would divide and split us up, it was going to be the area of our lives in which we were DIRECT OPPOSITES. John and I were at extreme opposite ends of the Christian spectrum are far as our religious affiliations were concerned. He was coming into the marriage from a very liturgical, structured, hierarchal church background and I was coming from a non-liturgical, loosely structured, Charismatic church background. Direct opposites!

As I write this book it's twenty-eight years later and I can honestly tell you, dear reader, that the Lord has been faithful! He has taken two completely opposite people and in the area of Christianity, he's molded us, molded us and united us. We are a beautiful composite of these two denominations! And, the rest of this book, dear reader, is devoted to telling you how He managed to accomplish that HUGE task! I hope you'll find it interesting...

Chapter Three

Ask And It Shall Be Given

"Ask, and it will be given you; seek, and you will find; knock, and it will be opened to you. For every one who asks receives, and he who seeks finds, and to him who knocks it will be opened." (Matthew 6:7-8)

Honeymooning in Hawaii was wonderful. John and I flew to Honolulu and then caught a commuter plane to Kawai, a small little island that afforded us an interesting study in "direct opposites". One side of the island was desert-like with cactus and other plants that survived without much rainfall, while the other side of the island was a virtual rain forest. In between was a mountainous sleeping volcano that managed to affect the island's weather enough to account for the differences in flora and fauna. A study in contrasts. A study in "direct opposites". How appropriate to begin our marriage!

A few days later we returned to Honolulu and since it was Sunday, we'd decided to take the city bus up into the hills overlooking the city to attend an Orthodox Church we found listed in the phone book. The morning had dawned sunny and warm. The clean-up crews had been out in force earlier and the streets and sidewalks were spotless. Shops and businesses had not yet opened for the day and only the song birds were up and awake! They greeted the beautiful day and filled the trees, everywhere!

We were the only people around as we scurried toward the bus stop. John "seemed on a mission to catch that bus" and I was doing my best to keep up with him when it suddenly occurred to me that we'd forgotten to set aside money for the inevitable "offering plate". John had no cash, nor did I; everything we had was in large denomination traveler's checks. "Oh, Lord," I said aloud, "forgive us, but we've forgotten to plan ahead and cash a traveler's check. All businesses are still closed and we have no money for the offering plate. Please forgive us!" Well, the words were barely out of my mouth when suddenly something blew toward me on the sidewalk. It was a five dollar bill!

Scripture says: "I the Lord search the mind and try the heart, to give to every man according to his ways, according to the fruit of his doings." (Jer. 17:10) And in Mark 11:24, we read, "Therefore I tell you, whatever you ask in my name, I will do it, that my Father may be glorified in the Son; if you ask anything in my name, I will do it." (John 14:13-14)

Praise the Lord in that He knows our heart's desires and our wishes even before we ask! He answered my prayer before it finished leaving my mouth!

There are many examples in Scripture that indicate the Lord desires us to ask him for things. In John 16:24, for example, it says: "Hitherto you have asked nothing in my name; ask, and you will receive, that your joy may be full." When we are "right with God," are repentant and humble of heart, and live within the will of God, he delights in answering our requests.

Chapter Four

My Thoughts Are Not Your Thoughts

"For my thoughts are not your thoughts, neither are your ways my ways," says the Lord. "For as the heavens are higher than the earth, so are my ways higher than your ways and my thoughts than your thoughts." (Isaiah 55:8-9)

I was about to learn that our prayer requests aren't ALWAYS answered as we hope for or desire.

The prospect of having a devout, Christian mother-in-law excited me. I'd always longed for someone who could be my "spiritual mentor" or advisor. So, after John and I were married, I began to call Mrs. Poulos on the phone and share with her some of the happenings I'd experienced through the Charismatic Renewal, a movement of the Holy Spirit that was sweeping through the United States in the late 1960's, early 1970's. I was "alive with enthusiasm" and eager to tell her about things I'd heard and miracles I'd witnessed. Expecting her enthusiasm to be synonymous with mine, I became confused when that didn't happen. Often, after silence from the other end of the phone line, I found myself saying to her, "Hello, hello, are you there? Did you hear what I just said? Did you hear what I just told you?" And, after another pause, the answer would come back, "Yes, I'm still here and yes, I heard what you told me."

I began to pray about it and I began to ask the Lord what was happening here. What was going on? Was it my fault that I wasn't making myself clear? Why was her reaction so unexpected and so unusual? Why, if Mrs. Poulos was "held in respect as being such a devout and inspirational Orthodox lady" was this happening? Why was there this breakdown in communications in the one area that should have united us and drawn us closer together?

I considered talking with my pastor or John's priest about the matter, but every time I thought about which man I should talk with I came to the conclusion that he'd tell me what he HAD to tell me, based on that clergyman's denomination. Pat answers. Answers that were "DENOMINATIONAL" and biased answers. Answers that they'd been schooled in saying to a parishioner such as myself.

I didn't want that, and so, as the saying goes, "I laid the problem on the Lord's altar". I went to my knees time and time again in prayer...asking Him to explain what was going on, religiously, in my mother-in-law's and my relationship. Oh, the weeping and travailing that went on as I beseeched the Lord for answers! And as the relationship worsened I grew more and more desperate. Every time I talked on the phone with her it was the same thing, the same "silence at the other end of the line" when I shared something religious. And, every time I attended John's church I felt like an outcast and a person whose faith and beliefs were even "wrong" somehow. It seemed expected that I would become Orthodox and even learn the Greek language.

There was never any inquiry about my beliefs nor my church involvements. Clearly, it was a taboo subject. Some times I even felt "ashamed" of my beliefs, as if, somehow, I were, indeed, a "heretic", which was the name I was even personally called by one priest. I was so amazed by being called this that I asked him to repeat what he had just said to me to make sure I'd heard correctly. Yes, he did, indeed, say that I was a "heretic!"

And still I "hung in there"...confused, but somehow steadfast! I had "experiential knowledge" that I'd received the Lord's special touch and anointing a year before. The subsequent events that had followed that "touch and anointing" convinced me that "it was real!" The Lord's presence and answers to prayer held me steadfast and I COULD NOT DENY WHAT I KNEW to be true! (Subsequently, 28 years later, I am convinced that the Lord had, in his infinite wisdom and mercy, given me that special touch and anointing to help me remain steadfast! Without it I am convinced that I might have forsaken Christianity in its entirety!)

John and I continued to attend both churches, every Sunday. My church had an 8:00AM service that gave me "spiritual sustenance" and allowed me to receive Holy Communion every Sunday. We'd get home from that church service around 9:20AM. I'd hastily prepare part of our dinner, set the oven on "timed bake," and we'd rush off to John's church, arriving about 9:50AM. While we always missed what's called "Matins" that began around 9AM, nevertheless, we were usually there for the beginning of the actual service, known as the "Divine Liturgy". This procedure we've observed to date, some 28 years! It's our routine for many Sundays.

In the course of the early years of attending the Orthodox Church, I had a heavy burden that the adults had little chance to grow spiritually. The Bible Study was poorly attended, the church library was sadly out of date, and there was no Adult Sunday School. Christian education seemed to pretty much end when young people graduated from high school. So, I started a book store. Out of our own money, I purchased several hundred dollars worth of Orthodox books and a cabinet on wheels (that John mounted on the cabinet) in which to store the books. Each Sunday I would roll the cabinet out of the corner of the social hall, unlock it, and place all of the books on three long tables for the parishioners to view when they came into the social hall after the Divine Liturgy. Silently, I prayed that people would purchase a book that might help them "walk a closer walk with the Lord".

My intentions were good and I greeted each onlooker with a big smile and a friendly word. Imagine my surprise when, from various angry lips I heard, "I thought Jesus chased the money changers out of the temple!" Though COMPLETELY SURPRISED, I hastily tried to set the record straight. "I'm not here to make money," I said. "These books were purchased out of my own money and they're here to help you in your walk with the Lord."

Well, I persisted Sunday after Sunday operating that book store. I'd carefully lay out all the books on the tables and then I'd go back into the Sanctuary to join my husband for the remainder of the Divine Liturgy. I was just beginning to see a small profit that would allow me to re-purchase books without spending more of my own money. Prayers were being answered! A few people were purchasing books!

The priest seemed delighted and enthusiastic about the book store's presence. Often during the announcements at the end of the Divine Liturgy, he reminded people that there were many fine Orthodox books there for purchase.

One Sunday, however, after I'd laid all of the books out on the tables, I placed the "book store money box" on the very bottom of the cabinet under some papers and books. It was completely hidden and there was no one in the social hall at that time to see me place it there. I felt it was safe. Nevertheless, in the short duration of barely an hour (while I attended the Divine Liturgy next door with John) someone went through that cabinet and took all of the money. I was devastated! Heartbroken! And thus the book store ended! I could not afford to keep purchasing books out of my own money! (A post script to this story goes like this: fast forward 26 years. The church has a new priest and has undergone a building renovation that relocated the priest's office on the second floor. This freed the former priest's office next to the Sanctuary and it has become a wonderful Orthodox book store! It is tended by a small group of parishioners who do all of the book purchases and maintain it! For this I Praise The Lord!)

Meanwhile, my church continued grow in its membership. A new, larger church was built in an adjoining suburb and the plan was that the church John and I'd been attending (and where I was a member) would dissolve into the new church. Such did not happen, however. Many of the members at the smaller, older church did not want to go to another, larger, church. The vote was cast and it was decided to keep BOTH churches operating and under the SAME NAME. Thus, in an unprecedented move, my church became a "two-campus church". Both churches would be staffed by the same group of pastors and they would "go between the two sites". In this manner BOTH CHURCHES GREW IN MEM-BERSHIP and today, as I write this, the church, North Heights Lutheran Church in Arden Hills and Roseville, Minnesota, has close to 8000 members and is what's called "a mega-church".

While it's Lutheran in affiliation, nevertheless, it has strong "Charismatic ties" and so no two Sunday services are the same. Not only do the pastors and the messages differ from Sunday to Sunday, but the order of the service differs each Sunday, as well. The services may, in addition to the pastor's message and Holy Communion, include bell ringers, a choir, a group of dancers, a personal testimony, a musical solo, or something else. And, it's quite normal to hear hand clapping, see arms and hands raised as people worship the Lord, and even hear "singing in the spirit" (which is singing in an ethereal sounding, but often unrecognizable language).

From this format it was often hard for me to "shift gears" and attend John's church. (It was hard for John, too.) There, each Sunday's service was pretty much the same and the Divine Liturgy followed the same basic format throughout the whole year.

Much of the Liturgy is spoken in Greek, as well as in English, and the use of incense, plus reverence of icons, making the sign of the cross and standing, sitting and behaving properly is strictly observed. In addition to a small choir, there are "chanters" who chant (a type of monotone singing) and stand in their designated spot in the front of the congregation.

Exact opposites on the spectrum, these two churches were about as opposite as you could get! And there John and I were...attending both, every Sunday!

One Spring I decided to volunteer at my church to help put together the scenery that's used for a play the church puts on every year, known as the "Passion Play...the story of the life of Jesus Christ." Each day I went to North Heights I'd paint scenery or help in the assembling of the huge set that was, eventually, to become "Jerusalem." Indeed, the entire front part of the Sanctuary became transformed! The section of seats where the choir usually sat became the "Upper Room" where Jesus and His disciples shared the "Last Supper" before his crucifixion. Above it, the balcony area became "Pilate's Court" where Pilate condemned Jesus to be put to death. Over on the other side of the Sanctuary, a whole section of seats became transformed into "Calvary's Hill" where Jesus was crucified.

20

One day while working on the set, the Director of the Play suggested that I might enjoy being IN the play! I'd never done any acting before and the thought of being in front of some 1200 people (25,000 people in the course of the 18 performances) rather frightened me. Nevertheless, the Director kept reassuring me that many in the cast of 450 people had never performed in a play before being in the Passion Play. She said things like "it will be a great experience" and "you'll love it...you'll see." Well, so O.K., I thought...I'll try it out!

And so, thus, it was the beginning of (at this writing) eight years of being an "extra" in the big Passion Play at North Heights. Over those eight years, some 144 performances, I've experienced so many blessings from my involvement! I've grown spiritually from reliving the words and events in the Bible. Scenes from Jesus' life come to mind countless times as I sit, either in John's church or in North Heights each Sunday, and hear the Scriptures read or listen to the sermons. It's helped make Jesus "alive and real" for me in a very personal way!

The Play has become important to me in other ways, too. I've made many friends at the church because of it and each year, as we reassemble and begin rehearsals, it's like a "homecoming," a chance to see people I haven't seen since last year's Passion Play. Some of the cast members are not members of North Heights, but come from other churches in the area. Some are Catholic, some are Baptist, some are from other denominations, but everyone comes together to share in the portrayal of Jesus' life.

It's also been a blessing for me to watch the countless children who are part of the cast. What a joy it is to watch as the children magically appear and "come running from every direction" to be in a particular scene. With one eye on a closed circuit TV monitor somewhere they've kept pace with the Play and in between scenes they've been busy with school homework, crafts and simple games. Suddenly, where just a few minutes before no one had existed...now, all of a sudden, everyone appears and the scene begins with everyone present and accounted for! Truly, my involvement in the Passion Play has been a rich experience with many rewards!

Sometime prior to 1981, a cry of my heart might have been stated in Psalms 119:125 and 144, where it says "I am thy servant; give me understanding, that I may know thy testimonies! Thy testimonies are righteous for ever; give me understanding that I may live, plus in Psalms 32:8 "I will instruct you and teach you the way you should go: I will counsel you with my eye upon you."

Clearly, the sovereignty of the Lord was about to be made known to me by an event that happened involving my mother-in-law. I was to learn that my understandings didn't go deep enough nor far enough and that the Lord needed to teach me, instruct me and counsel me because His thoughts are not our thoughts nor our ways His ways. As the heavens are above the earth, so are His ways higher than our ways and His thoughts above our thoughts.

As I stated earlier in this book, I couldn't figure out why my mother-in-law and I had been unable to talk about our different Christian beliefs, practices and experiences. When Catherine lived in Minneapolis, she suffered from a lot of health problems, many of which revolved around the fact that, as a young girl living in Russia, she'd contracted rheumatic fever and it had left her heart permanently damaged. She was a slight-of-build, frail woman who always said she was tired.

Since I'd been a part of so many Charismatic prayer and praise gatherings where healing miracles had been evidenced and since I'd laid hands on my friend Mike to be healed of hay fever and the Lord had answered our prayers, it seemed perfectly simple to me that what Catherine needed was to have hands laid on her and prayers for healing said. So, one day, when John and I visited his mother and sister, I suggested that we all gather round her and lay hands on her while we prayed for a healing.

Imagine my surprise when they did not join me in the "laying on of hands" and also, much to my surprise, nothing happened! They all just sat there looking at me. I was confused and devastated! No one had joined me in laying hands on her and praying for her. No one wanted a part in what I was doing. In fact, in the end, they all seemed MAD at me! The tension was "so thick you could cut it with a knife" and as John and I traveled home neither of us said a word.

The next day, I made an appointment for some counseling with my pastor about what I'd done. I needed help in understanding everything! Why had healing occurred for Mike and not for Catherine? And, even more perplexing, why were they all MAD at me?

My pastor gently reminded me that "God doesn't always answer our prayers…or at least He may not answer our prayers the way we want Him to answer them." He said, "Mike may have been healed because you were both in agreement about this healing and 'where two or three are gathered in my name, there am I in the midst of them'."(says the Lord, in Matthew 18:20). He also suggested that often the Lord will grant a prayer to be answered one time and not the next (for reasons only HE knows). Or, he suggested that maybe because I was such a new-born Christian when I'd prayed over Mike the Lord had honored that child-like faith and allowed a healing to increase my (and Mike's) faith in Him. But, the thing that my pastor said that impressed me the most was that MY HUSBAND HAD NOT REALLY CONCURRED IN WHAT I WAS DOING when I'd laid hands on his mother for healing! The methods I'd used were unfamiliar to everyone there except me as I not only prayed for healing, but spoke out against and called out the spirits of tiredness and weakness. My husband hadn't completely approved of what I was doing. Scripture says that the husband is the covering over the wife (Ephesians 5:23-33) and I'd gotten out from under that covering. I'd acted independently of him; we were not "of one accord" in laying on of hands and praying for her healing!

So, perhaps this one event, more than any other led to Catherine "closing the door on me," in a sense. In 1981, John's sister, Helen, and his mother, Catherine, moved to California and about a year later Catherine died. Before she and Helen moved to California, Catherine refused to discuss ANYTHING RELIGIOUS with me. Undaunted, I asked, "Could we just talk about ORTHO-DOX matters…the Orthodox Church and our attendance there." She said "No! I don't want to discuss anything religious with you!"

23

Well, so that ended it, the door was shut and unfortunately, it never opened again. We were never able to bridge the spiritual chasm that developed between us. I tried to keep the "communication lines open" by writing long and what I hoped were interesting letters to her, telling her what John and I'd been doing, plus whatever else seemed important at the time (except religious subjects). Since I'd always enjoyed writing...it was never a chore or task to be avoided. I enjoyed it! And, I hoped that, maybe, if she "got to know me better" perhaps she'd reopen that door. She never did. She moved and then died before we ever got this dilemma resolved.

Today, as I write this, because some 28 years have passed, I have to say that I've changed. Maybe you could say I've "matured spiritually", or maybe you could say I've become more "politically/spiritually correct." Maybe you could say I've "mellowed out." Maybe you could say I've become like other modern-day Christians. Maybe you could say a lot of things, but in my mind I feel sad, because gone is a lot of the FRESH, CHILD-LIKE FAITH I once had that's SO PRECIOUS! If I met Catherine today, and not back then, maybe I'd NEVER EVEN TRY to lay hands on her nor pray over her! Our relationship might not be problematic but, I think I would have missed out on SEVERAL valuable spiritual lessons!

At the outset of the relationship with Catherine everything was all very confusing. Nothing made sense. Soon, our relationship deteriorated. She shut the door and when she moved to California I often said I would have crawled across this country on my hands and knees if it would have made a difference in resolving our dilemma. Today, however, I know that I needed to learn the spiritual lessons my association with Catherine afforded me and to that end, I thank and praise the Lord for the entire experience! What it did for me, eventually, was to give insight into something far more widespread and extensive than our own personal relationship. We had had difficulty and indeed, never did bridge the spiritual chasm between us, but it only reflected what was going on across Christian denominational lines throughout the United States and indeed, the whole world during that time!

Chapter Five

Holy Spirit Led Revival

The Charismatic Renewal of the 1960's-70's in the United States caused many upheavals WITHIN mainline denominations, let alone what it did ACROSS denominational lines. Many Lutheran Churches split over the issue as some individuals and groups embraced it, while others in the same church didn't. Lutheran pastors embracing it were "ousted" or "replaced" when their congregations didn't approve. Many of the other Protestant (as well as some Catholic) churches were going through similar upheavals.

Once, in the early days of our marriage and while on a vacation, I told John that since I'd been unable to attend church on Sunday and since it was now Wednesday, I'd like to find a Charismatic church that had a mid-week prayer and praise service. Looking around town, the church we found had a sign out front that said "Mid-week service at 7:00PM." Thus, we were on hand as the service began. Unfortunately, it wasn't long before I nudged John and said, "I don't think this is the right church." Only a few other people were in attendance, but the first two rows of pews were fully occupied by a "goodly number of little old ladies". As the minister began his message on how the "Gifts of the Holy Spirit were for Apostolic Times Only," I whispered to John, "At the first opportunity, let's get out of here."

I was used to mid-week services, Protestant or Catholic, it made no difference, I'd attended both, that started at 7PM, had 500 people in attendance and by 10PM, no one wanted to leave. I was used to the gifts of the Holy Spirit being manifested and in evidence. I'd seen miracles. I'd EXPERIENCED and FELT the presence of the Lord! And here, in this "vacation" church was a minister who was preaching that these gifts were for Apostolic times only! POSH! Clearly we were in the wrong church!

Well, so gradually, I began to understand that not every Christian nor every Christian church embraced these "viewpoints about Holy Spirit manifestations". This was a surprise to me! These had become my viewpoints when I became a born-again Christian. I thought EVERYONE who claimed to be a Christian embraced these viewpoints.

When, over time, I began to see that some churches and some individuals thought otherwise or understood things differently than I did, I began to understand what the real problem had been between Mrs. Poulos and me. The Orthodox Church, John's church, was not a part of the Charismatic Renewal that swept through the United States in the 1960's-70's.

Nevertheless, one Sunday at St. Mary's Greek Orthodox Church in Minneapolis, a strange thing happened. John and I walked in, sat down, and I was instantly aware that there was a priest co-celebrating the Divine Liturgy whom I'd never seen before. When he spoke my inner spirit was quickened and it was like I somehow knew him! I nudged John and whispered, "Who is that priest? Do you know who that is? Listen to him…there is something distinctly different about him." Well, John didn't know who he was nor did he hear anything different about what was being said. He was speaking the words commonly spoken in celebrating the Divine Liturgy. Nevertheless, I was caught in rapt attention! Something was different about this priest!

Imagine my complete surprise when, at the end of the Divine Liturgy, that priest had an "altar call" at which he invited people from the congregation to come forward "to receive Christ anew and afresh into their lives!" People from all over the church went forward and stood in the front of the church! I couldn't believe what I was seeing! I was ecstatic and fell to my knees as tears…tears of joy…ran down my cheeks! The front of the church was full of people who'd come to receive Christ or to renew their commitment to Him! I couldn't believe this was happening in an Orthodox Church! An "altar call" with that format

NEVER happens in an Orthodox Church! But, then, and I'll never forget this part of that event, Mrs. Poulos, who always sat in the first row pew turned around to look back at the rest of the congregation. Our eyes met. There were tears in mine, but there was anger in hers! She clearly disapproved!

Well, subsequently, I learned the priest was, indeed, a Charismatic Orthodox priest with a small following of believers worldwide. He had a Charismatic newsletter to which I soon subscribed. His ministry, small though it was, flourished for many years.

Chapter Six

Heaven Bound

Many years before, in 1968, when I was twenty-eight years old, my father, Howard Daniels, had a heart attack and died. Dad and I had always been very close and his death devastated me. At that time, because I literally had no religion nor faith in God, I became angry at God. Why had He taken my father away from me at such an early age (he was 62)? I'll never forget what Mom and I did that first Christmas after Dad died. We had no family nor relatives who came to our side, no one who invited us to Christmas Day Dinner nor to celebrate in their festivities. It was "just the two of us" and so, since "going to church" meant little to us, we decided to attend a movie Christmas Eve. We thought "Fiddler on the Roof" would be a good choice, but we were really surprised when we realized that our "fellow movie theatre goers" were all Jewish believers. It was like a big party! Everyone seemed to know everyone else! And, there we sat, realizing that, somehow, we just didn't fit into this scene!

Dad's death had occurred about two years after his first heart attack. At the time of his first heart attack, I had completed teaching school one year in Michigan, but had returned to Hamline University (from where I'd graduated) for more classes that would entitle me to expand my degree so I could teach "core class" (a two hour block of time with the same students in English and American History). While attending Hamline again, I worked in the student dormitory as a dining room hostess to help offset the expenses of my tuition. One day, while in the dining room, I developed a "splitting headache unlike anything I'd ever experienced" and asked my boss if I could go home. I was sick.

As I began driving homeward, the headache began to subside and by the time I reached home, it was gone. When I got inside my home I found my father rolling around on the living floor in pain. Clearly, the Lord was in charge of my headache and it was He who'd made me go home. My father needed me! I took him to the doctor's office and then, when it was diagnosed that he was having a heart attack, I took him directly to the hospital where he was immediately attended.

That day, as I stood by my father's hospital bedside, I had a "word of knowledge" from the Lord. It was a clear message, so clear in fact, that it was just as if I'd turned on the radio. The message was, however, not about my father...it was about my mother. The message was "She will become more and more dependent on you!"

Dad was diagnosed as having had a heart attack. He should have had a heart by-pass operation, but the technology was such that the doctors gave him only a 50/50% chance of survival. The blockage problem was on the back side of the heart, an area hard to reach successfully.

Some time after my father had his first heart attack a very strange thing happened. One night he called me to the screened-in back door of our house and he said to me, "Do you see that star there?" I said, "What star, Dad, where?" "Right there, right where I'm pointing, don't you see that it's falling?" And, I said, "No, Dad, I don't see it!"

I've always wondered at that night's incident. Was there actually a falling star that he saw? Did he really see one? Was it a sign to him that "his days were numbered and he was like that falling star?" Or, was he, instead, trying to tell me that he thought his days were numbered, I don't know.

For some 32 years after my father had his second and fatal heart attack, I watched out for and included my Mom in every facet of my life. John and I expanded the second floor of our home to allow for a "mother-in-law apartment" for Mom and she lived with us for 18 years before she died.

In the year 2000, at the age of 91, my Mom died. We'd been a lot like sisters and while her death was hard on me, it wasn't nearly as hard as Dad's death had been. In the interim, I'd gotten over my anger at God for taking my Dad away, I'd accepted Jesus into my life as my Lord and Savior, my Mom had too, and together we'd grown in our understandings and beliefs in God.

Mom's health had declined in her latter years. First, she needed a hip replacement, then a knee replacement, then arthritis and osteoporosis caused a misalignment of her back and a lot of pain. Then, the replaced knee gave her a great deal of pain. Because it hurt so much to move, she did a lot of sitting and so the skin on her seat began to break down resulting in "bed sores". Congestive heart failure led to a swelling of her legs and "leakage of fluid through the skin." Bandaids were useless as the fluid seeped right through them. She grew continually unsteady on her feet and always sought my arm for balance. Several times when unattended, she fell down and this occurred because she needed the other hip replaced. That hip socket was so porous it was almost useless. Visits to the doctors became common place and I did my best to tend to her needs. Ultimately, however, it seemed as if 50% of my time was devoted to helping her in one way or another. For me it was very difficult to see such a strong, physically active body deteriorate so much. Every time I gave her a bath and washed her legs I would think about how strong they'd been when she was a city champion tennis player! And, I'd remember that she loved to tell the story of how she and dad had played 54 holes of golf every Saturday (without a golf cart! They walked!) when they worked at a summer job in Michigan before I was born. Then, after the 54 holes of golf, they'd go swimming in the evening.

As her health problems intensified, I was uncertain what to do for her. I prayed for her recovery and renewed strength. Many times I sought the Lord for wisdom on what to do. Many times I just didn't know what to do for her! She often said she was "tired of hurting" and I felt so sorry for her! Many nights I lay awake thinking, trying to figure out what I could do to help her. And, many nights I gave up and just cried.

Another problem was with her "eating." She had no appetite and "picked at her food." I began to prepare "special meals" for her in the hopes that she would eat more. Dinner time became something of an "ordeal" as she literally "dissected pieces of food and then spit out what she didn't want." Oh, it was difficult...for all of us!

Her advanced age was a problem in scheduling surgery for hip replacement and I didn't think she'd survive the surgery, anyway. Nevertheless, there didn't seem to be any other choice. Clearly, I couldn't continue to pick her up every time she fell down. She was too heavy for my own back! And so, we sought out a doctor who would agree to do the surgery and began to make arrangements for surgery, regardless of the consequences. It was a VERY stressful time for all of us!

She used to love to do "word search and number puzzles" and she had several subscriptions to puzzle books. She worked on them by the hour, believing that they "kept her mind active and helped her avoid old age dementia." She prayed to the end that she would be "mentally alert until the day she died." The Lord blessed her and answered that prayer! And while she lost interest in her puzzles toward the end of her life, nevertheless, I do believe that diligence with those puzzles DID help keep her mentally alert!

After months and months of dealing with her health and cleanliness problems, I reached a point whereby I was absolutely exhausted. It seemed to me as if I had to "think for two people" and I was really worn out. It was beginning to take a toll on me (as well as John). There seemed to be no solution. The problems were extensive and irreversible. And, one morning, in my prayer time, my quiet time before the Lord, I slumped into my chair and said to the Lord, "Lord, I don't know what to do for her. I can't do any more and really, you'd do us all a favor if you'd just let her go to sleep and not wake up. Let her wake up in heaven."

In my heart I believe that at that exact moment in time...the Lord took her home! I had what I'd call "an electric charge" shoot through my body and a little while later, when John and I called upstairs for her to come down for breakfast...there was no answer! I believe that that "electric charge" was the exact moment that the Lord took her home!

When we raced upstairs to her. There she was, sitting on her couch and she looked so peaceful...just like she was sleeping! She'd evidently gotten up that morning and had taken care of her bathroom chores, put her face makeup on and then sat down on her couch. A little while later...she died.

Some day, I'll see my mom and dad again. Some day they'll be there to greet me when I, myself, enter heaven. Some day, we'll stand there, side by side, along with the thousands and thousands of other Christians...followers of Christ down through the ages. Some day, I envision my dad on one side of me, my husband, John, on the other side, and my mom right in front of me and we'll stand there facing the Lord of Lords and the King of Kings as He sits upon His throne in heaven! And, the glory of the Lord will shine all around us. The glory of the Lord will be SO brilliant that no other light is needed, SO brilliant that if we were still in our mortal bodies our eyes would be blinded. And, the cherubim and the seraphim, the six-winged beings and the scores of angels will soar overhead. The "whir of their beating wings" will be heard everywhere. And, everywhere, there will be an additional ethereal sound as the "company of heaven" along with the people, the "bride of Christ", sing "Alleluia To The Lord of Hosts Who Sits on The Throne". You know, dear reader, as I think about it, it brings tears to my eyes because it will, indeed, be SUCH an awesome scene!

Chapter Seven

An Orthodox Cross to Bear

When John retired from his job at Deluxe Corporation, he began to spend more time at his church fixing things and often spent the better part of his days there. In time, because he often needed "an extra pair of hands" or added help, I went with him. I could "hold a board" while he nailed it in place, or "hold the ladder" while he repaired something near the ceiling. It was during one of these times that I looked around more closely and noticed that the Sunday School rooms, indeed, the whole Sunday School area, was "bland and uninteresting". There were few icons or other visual stimuli for the children, anywhere.

Young minds are like sponges and they need "visual input" whenever possible. I spoke to John about it and, with the approval of the priest, John and I purchased five new, large, bulletin boards that we mounted in the Sunday School hallway outside the classrooms. I became the "self appointed bulletin board lady" and began to create Christian, often strictly "Orthodox", themes for those bulletin boards.

I spent many, many hours developing the themes, the messages, and the artwork for the bulletin boards. I shopped the computer stores for clip art CD's that I could load into my computer to help me get the necessary artwork. Whatever I couldn't purchase, I often drew free hand or traced. I purchased background papers, borders, professionally produced pictures, icons, etc., and a variety of 3D materials, not to mention all of the glue and tapes necessary to do these bulletin boards.

Each month I tried to change all of the bulletin boards, making them coincide with the church calendar events. Starting in January and proceeding throughout the year, it was Theophany,

Great Lent, Annunciation, Pascha or Easter, Ascension, Pentecost, Transfiguration, Exaltation of the Holy Cross, and Christmas. Today, as I write this, I've been doing St. George's bulletin boards for several years and I've developed over 75 bulletin boards, not to mention countless free standing posters and several banners.

Why do I do it, you might ask. Why would I take the time and use personal money to do this for a church that I don't belong to and where I'm not a member. The answer's simple. I do it because I sincerely love the Lord, Jesus Christ, and I want those Orthodox children (and adults, as well) to also love him. Maybe, just maybe, if there's "visual stimuli 'round about" little children's minds (as well as adult minds) will be inquisitive and they'll want to know more about this Savior and Lord. Maybe they'll be inspired to ask questions and to inquire further. Maybe, just maybe, their Christian faith will be expanded and deepened.

Chapter Eight

Angels Unaware

My friend, Ellen, told me recently that she thinks I have a very good guardian angel. A very powerful angel who even carries a sword! I think she may be right. Throughout my life there have been many times when I've suspected as much because I've been protected in many ways, in many situations. I remember, just before 'ole weird Harold entered my life (during the dating years with Mike), when Mike and I were approached by some Mormons. They did their best to persuade Mike and I to come to one of their meetings. They showed us Biblical scriptures that we found interesting and some of their printed pamphlets. They seemed to show a genuine interest in us. We'd almost agreed to go to their meeting when 'ole weird Harold got a hold of us and prompted us to go, instead, to hear that blond-Afro-sporting-evangelist at his church. I believe that my guardian angel was on the job protecting me or I might have gone to that Mormon meeting.

My parents had strong guardian angels, too, I think. My dad often told the story about how, during the Great American Depression of the 1930's, when times were really tough, that they'd had an "unusual visitor" one day when there was a knock at their front door. The story went like this. Dad was working for the YMCA and the Y's finances were really low at that time. Dad had to take a cut in his salary. And, while his income wasn't much money, nevertheless, it was SOME money (which was more than a lot of people had at that time). Nevertheless, the bills still came due, the rent was due, gas needed to be bought for the car, food still needed to be put on the table, etc. One month, however, the expenses didn't equal the income and there was no money left to purchase food. The cupboard was bare. except for one can of cat food.

Mom and Dad looked at their cat and then at the can of cat food and wondered which, should it come to that, should they eat first.

Suddenly, there was a knock at the door and when they opened it there stood "a friend" holding a basket of canned goods and food. He said, "I thought you people might need this, so I brought it over."

The interesting follow-up to this story is that, even though that person looked exactly like a friend of theirs, when Mom and Dad, several days later, tried to thank him...that friend had absolutely "no knowledge of having done this deed!" He seemed to know nothing about the basket of food and canned goods! (Angels, unaware?)

In another favorite story of Dad's, he told how guardian angels were present. Mom and Dad owned a Model T Ford long before I was born and one day as they were driving along the highway, the car "lurched." Dad looked in the rear view mirror to see what he'd hit, but nothing was there. So, they drove on further and soon there were more "lurchings," each time followed by a smooth ride. Strange, they thought, but they kept going. Then, Dad, who was driving, saw a tire come rolling up beside the car. It passed the car and rolled on ahead of them before bounding off into the ditch. Dad said to Mom, "Hmmmm, will you look at that tire? I wonder who it belongs to. Looks like a good tire, too." So Dad stopped the car and got out to retrieve it and make it their own. Then he noticed why the car had lurched! It was THEIR TIRE and they'd been traveling along on only three tires! The car had stayed upright and traveled on three tires! (Angel help?)

During the Winter of 2002, my guardian angel worked overtime one day. Not having downhill skied for several Winters, I decided to "give it a go" after a beautiful snowfall blanketed the area in the fluffy white stuff. John went along and helped me buckle up my ski boots and tote my skis and poles to the "holding rail" before we went into the chalet for a cup of hot cappacino and a danish. As I sat at the table enjoying my hot drink, I felt something under my ski boot. Looking down, I thought it was a flattened, white plastic cup. I thought nothing more about it until

I got up to leave and took a step forward. My ski boot felt strange and, looking at the under side of it, I saw that that "flattened, white plastic cup" was actually a piece from the sole of my boot. Concerned, but determined to ski anyway, I headed for the "holding rail" to get my skis and poles before heading for the chair lift. Outside and almost to the rail, that boot literally "fell apart, piece by piece!" With each step I took more and more pieces of the boot fell off! And, finally, I was standing there in nothing but the INSIDE boot liner! The boot had disintegrated!

As I laughed at this ridiculous scene, I was well aware that if I'd gone up on that chair lift making it to the top of the hill, skiing down that hill would surely have resulted in SERIOUS injury. I would have had no control, whatsoever.

So, at the age of 60, (with "troubled knees" in my past) it was time to call it quits for downhill skiing. All the way home I praised the Lord and my guardian angel for protecting me! I could have been hurt very badly or perhaps, even killed.

Chapter Nine

Dreams

Today is May 2nd and as I write this part of the book, on this date 34 years ago, my Dad died. I can remember that day as if it was yesterday. As we sat across the breakfast table from each other I can remember thinking that he looked very tired. Really tired. It was two years since he'd had his first heart attack and in those two years he'd done nothing to change his living habits. I think maybe he COULDN'T CHANGE. I think it was hard for him to accept that he had a heart problem since physical fitness had always been SO important to him and so much apart of his life. I think maybe he thought that it wasn't as serious as the doctors claimed. I think maybe his health coverage wasn't sufficient to allow for such a big, expensive operation. I think maybe he even hoped that the problem would somehow "go away in time." At any rate, he had refused to have corrective heart surgery because the doctors gave him only a 50-50% chance of making it through the surgery and Dad said that the odds weren't good enough.

That morning, May 2nd, 1968, I went off to my job as a junior high school teacher and about mid-morning the Assistant Principal appeared at my classroom door. I took one look at the expression on his face and I think I knew what had happened. He said he'd take over my class and that I was needed at home, immediately.

The speedometer hit 80 miles an hour as I headed towards home on the freeway. But, then I said aloud to myself, "Slow down, Sue, he's already gone! No need to speed."

Mom and I suffered a great deal over the loss of Dad. We'd been a very close "three-some family." Oh, each of us tried to deal with it in our own way, but it was difficult and I think that neither of us accepted it very well.

I've never placed much value in dreams, but with the death of three individuals (my Dad, Mom, and first husband), I've had quite significant, quite unusual, dreams at night. In each case, three days after their passing I've dreamed these dreams. I tend to think that they were dreams "sent by the Lord" to help me cope. In the first dream involving my Dad, there was a "plexi-glass wall" between us. Dad appeared to be in a beautiful "meadow" on one side of this plexi-glass wall, and I was on the other side. My Dad was trying to tell me something. I pressed my ear to the plexi-glass and tried to hear what he was saying. I could not. I ran down the length of the wall trying to find an opening where I could hear him. I could not find such an opening. I stood still and tried to "read his lips". I could not. That's all there was to the dream, but the significance of it seems quite clear to me. Dad had always tried very hard to teach me and guide me regarding life's lessons and opportunities. He was a good father-figure and role model. It would have been very characteristic of him to "want to tell me something at that point in his experience". He would have wanted to "give me one last bit of counsel or advice".

The dream regarding my Mom, on the other hand, was quite different in nature. In that dream, I was awakened to hear Mom calling my name. I got up, went to the door to her upstairs apartment and opened it up. She was at the top of the stairs and she said, "Sue, I'm cold, can you get me some more blankets?" I went up the steps, took her arm and began to lead her down the hallway. That was the end of the dream. Here too, I think there was significance in the dream's message. I'd had that "message from the Lord" that day in the hospital when my Dad had his first heart attack and the message had been not regarding my Dad, but rather my Mom, and it was: "She will become more and more dependent on you." In those years since Dad's death I'd seen that come to pass. As the years had gone by Mom had, indeed, become more and more dependent on me and now, in death, it was little wonder that my dream reflected that fact.

The third dream I had was regarding my first husband. In this dream I was actually awakened in the middle of the night and he came into my mind. For some reason, I felt led to pray for him and so I did. It had been some 32 years since I'd been married to him. There'd been no contact with him, but that particular night I felt an urgency to pray for him and so I did. The next morning, I was sitting on the living room couch reading the newspaper when I turned to the Obituary notices and almost dropped the newspaper when I saw his death notice there. He had died three days before!

Well, so I don't know about dreams, but I do know that on these three occasions in my life, they were very significant! I've come to believe that, yes, the Lord does sometimes speak to us out of the depths of our dreams!

Chapter Ten

Remember The Sabbath

"Remember the Sabbath day, to keep it holy. Six days you shall labor, and do all your work; but the seventh day is a Sabbath to the Lord your God: in it you shall not do any work, you, or your son, or your daughter, your manservant, or your maidservant, or your cattle, or the sojourner who is within your gates;" (Exodus 20:8-10).

Scripture also says; "My son, do not regard lightly the discipline of the Lord, nor lose courage when you are punished by him. For the Lord disciplines him whom he loves, and chastises every son whom he receives." (Hebrews 12:5-6).

Some time before I'd become a Christian the Lord had impressed on me the importance of keeping the Sabbath day holy. I'd read a book about a professional golfer that had chosen to forego fame and fortune because golf circuit tournaments usually conclude on Sunday. That man's devotion to his faith impressed me! He believed that the Sabbath should be kept hallowed and holy.

Retail stores (once closed on Sundays when I was a young girl) were permitted, in the 1960's to be open on Sundays and it was business as usual, seven days a week. Besides that, I observed that neighborhoods were alive with the sounds of homes being remodeled, garages being built, and lawnmowers cutting grass. Women hung out the family wash, while men washed cars. What had happened to the practice of keeping the Sabbath day holy? If God had created heaven and earth, the sea, and all that's in them in six days, but rested on the seventh, what gave mankind the idea that the seventh day of the week could be treated like any other?

Early-on in my Christian walk I'd decided to honor the Sabbath, to keep it holy and to abstain from work. Nevertheless, one Sunday before the beginning of an especially busy week, I decided to bake two pies. I was going to "get the jump on a busy week!" You've heard the phrase "easy as pie?" Well, that was the case with my lemon meringue and banana cream pies. The recipes were almost memorized and these pies turned out well every time. I'd made these pies MANY times!

This time, however, even though the ingredients were correct and my procedures the same as every other time, BOTH pies FLOPPED! I have to conclude that the Lord wanted "to remind me" that the Sabbath Day is to be kept holy!

Time passed and there was another time when I didn't observe Sunday as a day of rest. I decided to wash clothes. What harm could there be in "throwing in a load of wash and letting the washer do its thing?" Other people did it all the time. I'd just let the washer and drier do the work. Surely, there couldn't be any harm in that! Nevertheless, I should have known that the usage of modern, automated machines did not alter the meaning of those words in Exodus, "…the seventh day…in it you shall not do any work."

That day, about mid-cycle through the wash, the machine stopped. No unusual noise, no indication that anything was wrong, it just stopped! The clothes were partially washed, but remained in two feet of water. I had to fill the laundry tubs with water and finish washing the clothes by hand. Clearly, I was getting the Lord's message again. I knew I had not kept Sunday a day of rest nor had I kept it hallowed and holy.

Sometimes, the Lord permits trouble to strengthen us spiritually. Sometimes, the word "discipline" enters into the picture. The Lord has to "discipline us", to build up our self control, proper conduct, and realization that, if we're going to follow Him, we must acknowledge Him in ALL things and at ALL times! We must obey His word and in this case, He said to "remember the Sabbath and to keep it holy." To this day, some 30 years after becoming a born again Christian, my husband, John, and I adhere strictly to this practice! We don't work on the Sabbath!

42

Chapter Eleven

I Will Never Fail You

"It is the Lord who goes before you; he will be with you, he will not fail you or forsake you; do not fear or be dismayed." (Deuteronomy 31:8)

And in Hebrews 13:5, we read, "I will never fail you nor forsake you."

John had been away on business and after five days, I could hardly wait to meet him at the airport. As I traveled the twenty miles to the airport, I reminisced about some of the things we'd done together, our good times, how fortunate I was to have such a good husband and how good our years of marriage had been.

Suddenly, my happy thoughts ended as a bright red light appeared on the dashboard signaling car trouble. To make matters worse, in my daydreaming, I'd taken a wrong turn. I was headed for downtown Minneapolis instead of the airport. Now the trip would be longer than usual.

I knew that whenever a trouble light appears on the dash that it's best to stop the car, but the freeway was dark and as I surveyed the exit ramps for a service station, there were none.

The car's power began to wane. The headlights and the lights on the dashboard began to dim. The engine began to "miss" and seemed about to stop completely. Silently, I began to pray "Help me, oh, Lord, please help me!"

The lights on the dashboard went out completely and the engine missed for longer and longer periods of time. "Just a little further," I prayed.

Remembering that parking spaces at the airport were always at a premium, I prayed right out loud that a place would be available. "Please let there be a spot, Lord! This car can't go much farther, Lord!"

I was barely into the lot. There! Over there! Is that a spot?

As I pulled into that parking space it was as if the Lord's hand was taken off the car's engine; it went silently and completely dead.

Few husbands have ever looked as good to their wives as mine did to me that night. Amidst tears, I gave thanks and rejoiced...I had my husband back home safe and sound and I'd made it to the airport! "Great is our Lord and greatly to be praised." (Psalm 48:1)

John had always been blessed with a knowledge of how to fix things. He loved the challenge of trying to figure out what was wrong. So, while I described the car's behavior, he began checking out the possible trouble spots.

In not much time at all John narrowed the possibilities down to one, a faulty starter solenoid. Then, by taping the problem area with a little tape he always carried in the glove compartment and by getting an engine "jump" from the airport tow truck, we were on our way home.

And, I can recall another time that the Lord showed us that he is always with us and will never fail us. This time, John and I narrowly missed being in a serious automobile accident. It was so close that even now, years later, I can still recall it! I'll never forget it!

We had been to an evening Bible study at his church and were about to begin our journey home. The church's parking lot descends a hill onto a very busy thoroughfare of traffic. After checking for approaching traffic and seeing none, John eased the car onto the thoroughfare. Suddenly, seemingly out of nowhere, a speeding car appeared. We were headed for what appeared to be a pile up, as well as possible injuries as the speeding car was about to collide with our car on the passenger's side. With little more time than we could utter the words, "Oh, Lord!" the approaching car swerved, jumped the curb onto the boulevard, narrowly missed a lamp post and a street sign by going between them and then swerved back onto the street, ending up in the

44

same lane and line of direction as before. Not only had that driver miraculously missed hitting our car, but he'd managed to miss hitting everything else as well. We drove around the block hoping to thank that driver for his quick reflexes and excellent driving, plus pay for damages to his car when he hit the curb, but by the time we got back to the spot where it had happened, neither the driver nor his car was anywhere to be found!

Countless other times the Lord has proven himself faithful. Once on a shopping spree in downtown St. Paul, Mom and I drove around block after block looking for a parking space. Only after we prayed did a spot materialize and it do so immediately. The Lord wants to be asked so he can show us his faithfulness.

As we got out of the car, I put seventy-five cents into the parking meter when we remembered that it was a holiday and there was free parking. We'd paid for parking, needlessly. But, the Lord took care of that, too. As we were about to begin our shopping, a dollar blew toward us along the sidewalk. The Lord had not only provided us with a parking space, but he had refunded the money we'd mistakenly fed into the meter, and, in abundance, too. Truly, as Deuteronomy 31:8 says, the Lord goes before us and he is with us, he will not fail us.

On another occasion, however, I wondered if the Lord was with us or not. In this situation, after several years of marriage, John and I felt that because my Mom wasn't "making ends meet" each month, financially, and aging was making cleaning her apartment difficult, plus, her meals weren't as nutritious or balanced as they should be, maybe we'd have to build a "mother-in-law apartment" upstairs in our house. So, we hired a contractor to rough-in an upstairs dormer on the south side of our house and our goal, albeit, it ultimately took five years to complete, was to build an upstairs apartment for her.

The day the contractors arrived to remove half of the roof, the weatherman said there was only a 35% chance of rain.

From the windows of the Christian church where I was working that day, I could see that that 35% chance had turned into a reality. It was a downpour!

Hoping to find prayer support from my fellow staff members and finding none (I was surprised when they actually made fun of and joked about my concern!), I asked to go home to help my husband cover the floor of the upstairs so that we wouldn't lose our house to the downpour. If water got into the insulation between the walls or got through the upstairs floor into our downstairs ceiling, it would be disastrous.

When I arrived home, I could see that the builders were frantically working to get the new roof over most of the house.

Mom (bless her heart!) was interceding in prayer for the Lord's help and John and I prayed right out loud as we rushed around soaking up puddles of water with towels and newspapers before covering the areas with plastic. Perhaps, the builders prayed too, as we'd hired a Christian building company to do the work.

When everything was over and done with, our house was saved that day! We were fortunate. But, I learned a valuable lesson that day, people may fail you, even Christian people, but God is faithful and He will NEVER fail you nor forsake you!

In the Spring of 1998 I was reminded of that fact again. John and I were eagerly awaiting the visit of some friends from Germany. They were coming to spend a month with us and in that month we planned to show them not only Minnesota's highlights, but the Black Hills of South Dakota as well as the Colorado Rockies. John had met Heinz when he was stationed with the U.S. Army in Germany back in the late 1950's. Their friendship had endured some forty years or so.

One day, in Kitzingen, Germany, John had left his Army unit to go into town and was standing outside a movie theatre trying to decide what the movie on the marquee was all about when some young Germans came along on their way to that movie, also. John asked them, "Do any of you guys speak English? Can any of you tell me what this movie is all about?" One German, Heinz, said yes, he spoke English and if John wanted to come along into the theatre, he would do his best to translate the movie for him.

After the movie, Heinz invited John to his home so he could meet his family. From that beginning, when both men were about

46

20-23 years old, a friendship developed and over the years, every year at Christmas time, the two men exchanged Christmas cards and letters that brought each other up to date on the year's happenings in their lives.

As a young man, after being stationed a short time in Kitzingen, John was transferred to Frankfurt and the two men never saw each other again until 1993 when Heinz and his wife, Sieglinde, came to the United States to visit Sieglinde's uncle who lived near Boise, Idaho. John and I decided that we couldn't let that opportunity go by, so we flew out to Boise and spent some time with them. When we drove up to the uncle's home, there was Heinz standing on the curb awaiting John and the two men embraced each other as if they were long lost brothers! It was really touching to see this reunion after so many years!

Now, in 1998, five years later, Heinz and Sieglinde were flying into Minneapolis to come and visit us. We were SO excited!

With only a week to go before they were due to arrive, John and I had cleaned and prepared our home and yard until it was near-perfect. Everything was ready!

Suddenly, one day, the weather report didn't sound good. There was an intense storm approaching our area. High winds with near-tornado velocity, along with large hail stones, were expected. The clock indicated it was 4:30 P. M., but it was so dark that the street lights went on. There was an eerie silence and a greenish color to the sky. And, then it hit! The hail stones pelted the windows and we thought they were going to break. The wind whipped the tree branches to and fro until almost horizontal. All at a once there was a loud "thud!"

"What was that?" I asked Mom, to which she replied, "A door slammed shut somewhere!" I thought to myself as I raced upstairs, two steps at a time, "No, that was much worse than a door slamming shut. I hope it isn't what I think it is! Oh, Lord, no! No! Please, not what I think it is!"

I looked out of the upstairs window and...yes...it was as I had anticipated. The huge Basswood tree in our backyard had been uprooted by violent straight line winds and had toppled over and crashed through the roof into our house!

I raced back downstairs shouting to John and Mom about what I'd seen and together we gathered on the back porch to look at the damage! Our back yard was a mess! Leaves, branches and debris everywhere! Worse yet, the roof of our house had tree branches sticking out from it!

"Quick!" I shouted, "we MUST call someone to help with the tree removal before businesses close for the week. It's Friday and tomorrow morning will be too late! We must call someone NOW!" And, so we scanned the pages of the phone directory for a tree removal company that could help us. "Help us, O Lord!" I prayed. "We need your help, and we need it now, O Lord!"

Finding a company, John called and instantly, as though he'd been sitting there awaiting our call, the phone was answered by the owner! It was almost 5:00 P.M. Another few minutes and it would have been too late! He said he was just about to leave for the day! (Thank you, Lord, that we acted so promptly and that you heard our prayers for help!)

John explained the situation to him and the owner said he'd come out immediately to take a look at the damage. Sure enough, within a short time he arrived. He took one look at the uprooted tree and said the job would necessitate a crane to remove the tree from the house. He'd have to rent one. So, he said he'd be back the next morning, at 9:00 A.M., with his crew and equipment.

Sure enough, true to his word, bright and early the next morning, he and his crew went to work with power saws, stripping the tree of branches. All branches were cut off the main trunk and then, with the use of a crane, the main trunk was pulled away from the roof and the house. Then, he covered the damaged roof with a big piece of blue plastic tarpaulin and nailed it securely in place.

Thus, it was that one week later, Heinz and Sieglinde arrived, but alas, our "perfect home and yard" was no longer that...it looked like a disaster zone! The trunk of the tree was still standing upright about two feet from the house (awaiting still other equipment that could saw that huge trunk into smaller pieces plus remove them), the roof was covered with a blue plastic tarp, the driveway was destroyed, and our back yard had a big hole where the tree had been before toppling over.

Nevertheless, we rejoiced that we'd been SO blessed by the Lord! He'd heard our prayers and had answered our cries for help. The tree had been removed off of our house, the house was "buttoned up" and was safe from the elements, the driveway could be repaired and dealt with later, as well as the big hole and root system of the tree. Our property had been secured. It was safe...and so were we!

The Lord was SO GOOD to us! We got help, immediately! And, we soon learned that the ravages of that storm left some people with far worse situations than ours had been. The wide spread damage forced people to clean up their properties for months and months afterwards. Tree removal companies such as the one we'd called were "back logged with work." Work schedules were full and people had to put their disasters on hold until help could come to them. We had been SO fortunate!

Because the tree crashed through the roof of our house, our insurance covered most of the damages. We were also blessed in that the tree landed BETWEEN the studs of our house. Had it landed ON a stud, or studs, it would have driven those boards vertically down into my kitchen and the damage would have been far worse! There would have been structural damage. But, it was as though "someone" had guided that tree to fall "perfectly" BETWEEN the studs and those studs were only 16 inches apart! Amazing!

With the house buttoned up safely under a plastic tarp and the tree trunk awaiting a future time when it could be sawed apart and disposed of, we packed up our car, took our suitcases and Heinz and Sieglinde, and went away on our preplanned vacation! We were off to the Black Hills of South Dakota and the Colorado Rockies to show our German friends a good time!

Another time I was also reminded of the fact that "God is faithful and He will never leave us nor forsake us." He is always there for us.

Each year, my church observed the 4th of July by staging a "Freedom Celebration". Three church services right before the 4th paid homage to this nation's founding fathers and mothers, as well as present day men and women who had served in the armed forces. It was a very patriotic pageant!

Mom had been after me for years to perform in the Freedom Celebration and do a flag twirling routine my father had taught me as a kid. I'd always declined, but the year after she died I couldn't shake the idea of performing that routine! I don't know if Mom was up there pushing me to do it or not, but I soon contacted the director and his wife and showed them the routine. When they saw it they were impressed to the point that they wanted me to do it "in the center spotlight". So, dressed in a navy slack suit and holding two large American flags, I was to begin the drill slightly to the right of center stage while each branch of the armed forces was acknowledged and the men and women in the audience from that branch stood up. Then, when all branches had been acknowledged, I was to stop my drill, walk to center stage and complete the drill as everyone paid tribute to our country's flag and the "Stars and Stripes" by John Philip Sousa resounded in the background. It was a fitting ending to a "military salute of the armed forces!"

While I'd known the routine since being a kid, it had been many years since I'd performed before a large audience of people. Performing this solo number before some 1500 people had my knees knocking! I was shaking so badly that I thought I was going to fall down. I was so afraid that I'd drop one of the flags, get one of them tangled up, or make a mistake in the routine. But, I kept a big smile on my face and acted as though doing this drill was a common every day occurrence for me!

Silently, as I counted out the movements and did the drill, I prayed, "Oh, Lord, help me! Be with me!"

There were three Freedom Celebration performances, one Saturday night and two on Sunday morning, and all three proved successful. The Lord had proved faithful once again and I successfully completed all three performances without any flaws!

Immediately, people began congratulating me, asking where I'd learned this drill and how my wrists and arms could ever accomplish such movements. By the end of the third performance, I was even being asked if I could perform it in conjunction with a July 4th celebration at a local park and as part of entertainment at a nearby nursing home for senior citizens.

It felt wonderful to be in demand and popular! It was my moment of glory!

That night at home, however, something happened that made me wonder if the Lord, who'd been there for me, who'd certainly been faithful and had heard the fearful prayer of my heart...hoping that I'd perform that drill perfectly...didn't also have a keen sense of humor!

The phone rang and it was a man from my church, a man who's name I knew, but whom I'd never spoken with before. He asked me a very unusual question. He suggested that there was some paint on the ceiling and walls of one of the rooms at the church that they needed to have "power washed". He suggested that the job would involve some ladder work, but that it shouldn't pose too much hardship on the person doing the job. He sounded quite sincere and really desperate to find someone to do this task. He apologized for having to ask me. He wanted to know if I would volunteer to do this task!

Imagine my surprise! Here, not eight hours since my "shining moment in the center spotlight" I was being asked to volunteer to clean paint off the walls and ceiling! Talk about landing back in reality with a thud! That did it!

I wondered if it was some sort of a joke, but he sounded so sincere that, to this day, I think it was a legitimate phone call and request! Nevertheless, at age 60, I felt that I was just a little too old to undertake such a physical task and so I graciously declined.

Afterwards, when I'd hung up the phone, I couldn't help laughing! The Lord, in his infinite wisdom, had not allowed me to "stay puffed up with center spotlight mentality" very long. He'd humbled me and brought me back to reality quickly, but the timing of it was, as is always the case with the Lord, absolutely PERFECT! John and I laughed about it for days afterwards!

Chapter Twelve

It's A New Day

Another practice that John and I have adhered to since first married is that we start our days with "a time of prayer." You've heard of a "prayer closet", perhaps, and that's exactly where John goes for his time of prayer...his own personal clothes closet! He shuts the door to the bedroom and goes into his prayer closet. Meanwhile, I close the door to the spare bedroom where I meet the Lord in my "quiet time of prayer." When we're on vacation away from home, we alter our places for this time of prayer, but we never start the day without it! Over the years, it's been "mandatory" and we wouldn't think of facing our days otherwise. As we face the outside world, with all of its trials and tribulations, we ask, each day, that the Lord guide, direct and protect us. And, come what may, we know He's there for us and with us!

In the year 2002, at the age of 67, the Lord was really there one day for John when he was walking around the Lake. On this particular day, John had gone by himself as I had other things to do. The day was windy and John had to stop several times to "catch his breath." Even though wind might have been a factor, nevertheless, this need to stop was unusual and the next day, John (who rarely went to the doctor for any reason!) called the doctor and made an appointment. Something was definitely wrong! Within days a treadmill stress test was scheduled and John promptly flunked it! A radioactive isotope test and dye injection further revealed that he had blocked arteries and needed a quadruple heart by-pass operation. (John's father and his father's two brothers had all died of heart attacks just about the age of John. Heredity was clearly a factor!)

John's tests revealed that there were 10 spots of blockage in the arteries of his heart, with the most serious a 90% blockage of the left main coronary artery. Right where that big artery divides, both branches of the artery had serious blockages. And, because of the location of that blockage, open heart surgery was the only option available. So, from diagnosis to day of surgery, it was one week! Everything happened SO quickly!

At John's church, the Priest anointed him with oil and prayed over him. Then, I called my church and put John (and the doctors) on the prayer chain. The Sunday before surgery, after the service, I slipped information about the date and time of the surgery into the Pastor's hand. Two churches, double coverage! We needed all the "prayer help" we could get!

The prayers began to work because as John neared the day of surgery, both of us had a definite inner peace about it and we felt confident that all would go well. Nevertheless, personally, for me, I wondered if I could "handle it." I knew the Lord was with us, but somehow I wondered if I didn't need a "skin-on person," too. Someone who would stay with me in the house and be there for me when I went home late at night from the hospital. I prayed about it and asked the Lord what He thought.

I'd told Ellen (a gal I'd become friends with through the Passion Play at my church) that I was a bit apprehensive about staying alone, especially the night right after John's surgery. Well, the Lord spoke to Ellen's heart and she not only came down to the hospital the day of the surgery and spent the whole day with me, but actually "moved into our home" and stayed a week...until after John was back home again!

It was a 5 1/2 hour operation and during that time both heart and lungs were shut down with a heart-lung machine keeping John "alive." When it was all over and he was in the Intensive Care Unit, I went looking for him. It had been a long day of waiting and I was anxious to see him. Nevertheless, if I'd waited in the Waiting Room like I was supposed to do I might have spared myself some grief and anxiety. I wouldn't have seen what I saw! They'd just wheeled John into the ICU; his eyes were still taped shut, he was still strapped to the bed. Two nurses tended to his medications and watched the monitors for results, along with noting his blood pressure and heartbeat.

Gradually, over the next several hours, he began to "wake up" and come out of the anesthesia. The tape had been removed from his eyes, but his lids were still sticky and he had trouble opening them. He was still strapped to the table and the tube was still down his throat. There were tubes sticking out from all over his body. I was O.K. with that, but when he did something that "was so uniquely characteristic of my dear husband, something that perhaps only he would do"…well, "I lost it." My heart cried! I almost fainted! John, with eyes still shut and that tube still down his throat, tried to raise himself up and with a LOT of effort and a GREAT deal of stress, said, "I just want to…thank everyone."

What a dear man! That was so like John…always thinking about the OTHER person! Always thinking about their welfare and worrying about them!

A day after Ellen went home and it was "back to just John and me around the house" I was in the kitchen doing the dishes. With a dish and the dishtowel in hand, I went into the living room to check on John. He was sitting on the couch watching TV, but was clutching to his chest his "heart shaped pillow" they'd given him in the hospital. All of a sudden his head shot backwards, his eyes closed, his arms went rigid against his sides and his whole body began to convulse. I ran for the kitchen phone and called 911. The paramedics came. But, by the time those four paramedics came into the living room, John was "back with us" and he seemed to be O.K., again. They checked his vital signs, gave him an electrocardiogram and said that, undoubtedly, he'd experienced "a pain spasm," the result of coughing while I'd been in the kitchen. A trip to the hospital didn't seem necessary and they thought he'd be alright. Nevertheless, the episode had "sent me into orbit" and for awhile there I'd thought I'd lost him!

The Lord proved faithful through the whole surgery and subsequent recovery period. There were a few rough times, but both John and I saw the hand of the Lord at work, from beginning to end. He'd gotten John to see a doctor (that, in itself, was a miracle, for he seldom went to a doctor for ANY reason!) before there'd been a heart attack. No heart damage had occurred. And, the by-pass operation had gone well, there'd been no incidents nor complications. Also, the Lord had sent me Ellen, the right person for the situation. She was a person who gave me both the physical and spiritual encouragement and attention that I needed.

Chapter Thirteen

Love Him With Your Whole Heart

This year, as I write this, it's over 30 years since I gave my life to Christ. Thirty years since I said, "Lord, I want to go ALL the way with you. I want to lay my ALL on your altar! I know that I'm a sinner and I ask that you forgive me for my thoughts, words and deeds, anything that doesn't please you. I need you in my life and I ask that you come in and be my Lord and Savior, FOR EVER AND ALWAYS!"

My dear reader, I have to tell you with all sincerity, the Lord has been SO FAITHFUL! SO EVER PRESENT for me! I've been SO BLESSED! And, as I praise Him, I have to say that I am SO GRATEFUL!

When I think back over the years about how I became a born-again spirit filled Christian, my marriage to John, the subsequent uncertainties and confusions regarding "life 'tween two denominations" at opposite ends of the Christian spectrum, the lessons I've learned, the melting and molding that's gone on in my life (and John's), I have to say that it's been an "interesting journey." A journey that goes onwards; a journey that's not over yet.

What I can tell you after these thirty years, dear reader, is that, overall, I've learned ONE VERY IMPORTANT LESSON, one important lesson that makes everything else pale by comparison. One lesson that I'd like each person reading this book to "take to your heart" and "make it your own word of advice." That lesson is simply this: If you, as a follower of Christ, are DEAD SERIOUS about following Him, if you remain true to Him, repent of your sins and seek Him daily, if you spend time with Him every day in earnest prayer, if you "don't dabble in" or become involved in anything He disapproves of, if you talk to

Him about nearly everything in your life...every day, and, MOST IMPORTANT...if you LOVE HIM WITH YOUR WHOLE heart...He will become your best friend and confidant as well as your Lord and Savior. He will never leave you, nor forsake you and come what may in your life, good or not so good, He'll see you through it, He'll be there for you every step of the way! He'll attend to all of the little details and those details will be taken care of "way beyond chance or happenstance." He'll provide for you as He sees fit and in the ways He knows are best for you!

As Christians, many of us tend to make our religion way too complicated and structured. Many of us like to "intellectualize or philosophize Christianity." Many of us think that we must adhere to strict hierarchal dogmas and that we must "DO" thus and so in order to find favor with the Lord. Many of us are either "scared stiff" of the Lord or feel He's somehow "too lofty" for us to approach; so we seek Him via going to the Saints or the Virgin Mary, FIRST. The end result may be the same thing, but beware of "detours!" There are, alas, many detours and we must always be mindful, lest we take a detour and fall into a trap!

The GREAT AND FIRST COMMANDMENT that Christ gave was this: "You shall love the Lord your God with all your heart, and with all your soul, and with all your mind." (Matthew 22:37 RSV). To that end, I've tried to live my life and so far, I haven't regretted it for one minute!

Epilogue

Susanna

About ten years after becoming a born again Christian, I learned that even our names have special significance in the sight of God. My name, it seems, was foreordained to be Susanna, or Susan. In Luke 8:1-4, we read that as Jesus went on a tour of the cities and villages of Galilee to announce the coming of the Kingdom of God, he took along his twelve disciples, plus several women, several from which he'd cast out demons or healed. The Scriptures record the names of three of these women, Mary Magdalene, Joanna, and Susanna. Susanna was one of the women whom Christ healed both physically and spiritually and who went on to reveal her gratitude by ministering unto Jesus and his disciples.

In Romans 12:6-8, we read about the seven motivational gifts of the Holy Spirit. They include the gifts of prophecy, teaching, exhortation, giving, organizing, having mercy and serving others.

Susanna had the gift of serving others and undoubtedly derived a great deal of joy from serving her Lord and Master, Jesus Christ, and his disciples.

One of the characteristics of a person with a motivational gift for serving others is that they derive a great deal of joy when their serving frees the other person to accomplish important tasks. Thus, it was that as Susanna ministered unto Jesus and his disciples that they, in turn, were freed to heal and deliver the sick, plus teach and proclaim the message of salvation and eternal life.

In my own life there have been many times when I've been quite joyful as I've served others and this, in turn, freed them to accomplish some important task. Many times when my husband, for example, was hard at work fixing or repairing something, he realized that in order to finish the job a new part or a tool needed to be purchased. Without hesitation, upon learning this, I'd volunteer to dash off to the nearest hardware store to purchase it. It didn't even matter that I might be "right in the middle of something." Serving others is a God given quality and it's just part of the person's nature.

God has foreordained each person's gifts and has placed at least one within each of us. To the degree that we know of this and use it, we please God and ourselves.

DEVOTIONAL READINGS

Introduction

This devotional section is included to help you grow in your relationship with your Lord, Jesus Christ. There are only seven daily devotions, but it's hoped that if you don't already begin your day with a quiet time of prayer, Bible reading and worship, that, in the course of a week (using one of these devotions each day), you'll begin the habit of doing so and when you've concluded this section you'll see the need to continue this daily practice and will search out other materials for your daily quiet time.

Some of these devotions are based on a book my father was working on shortly before he died in 1968. His objectives were different than mine as, being in Y.M.C.A. work, he was targeting youth. He envisioned writing devotions for camp counselors, club leaders, or possibly church groups and hoped that the devotions presented in his book could be used to conduct interesting youth devotions and discussions with a minimum amount of study and effort on the part of the leader.

Thus, some of the ideas and content of these devotions have been taken from his book and it's with a great deal of respect and admiration for him that I've included them in this section of my book.

An Old Wire Basket

A young man asked an old lady if she'd been to church on Sunday. The old lady replied, "Yes, I have been. In fact, I was there twice, once in the morning and once in the evening."

Impressed, the young man asked the old lady what the morning sermon had been about.

"Well," said the old lady, "Let's see…what was it about?" She thought for a moment and then said, "I guess I can't really remember what it was about. It was a good sermon, but I just couldn't remember the message."

Again the young man asked the old lady, "What was the text and the sermon in the evening service?"

Again the old lady thought for a moment and then said, "I'm afraid I can't remember that either."

Somewhat exasperated, the young man asked, "What's the use of going to church if you can't remember the text or bring home some knowledge of the sermon?"

After a moment's pause, the old lady picked up an old wire basket and asked the young man if he would take it, fill it with water and bring it to her.

"Oh, come now," said the young man, "I'm not stupid. You know as well as I do that there wouldn't be a drop of water left in the basket by the time I brought it back to you."

"Perhaps you are right," replied the old lady, "but I dare say that the basket might be a little bit cleaner."

So it is with daily devotions. Beginning your day with a quiet time filled with prayer, Bible reading, a daily reading and worship carries our thoughts upward toward God. It focuses our thoughts on a higher level and gets us closer to God. Like the old lady's church attendance, while she couldn't remember the sermons, nevertheless, she knew she was "a little bit cleaner," a little closer to God, because she'd spent that time with Him.

When we begin our day with a quiet time before the Lord (devotions), sometimes we're feeling apathetic, rushed for time, even devoid of any desire to do this activity. This is not unusual. We all lead busy and full lives.

Nevertheless, think about an airplane taking off. As you watch it rise, a sensation gives buoyancy to your body and it seems as though you can almost "take off with it." You "rise with it" and swoop your arm in an upward path to imitate the plane's rising. Or think about getting into an elevator. As the elevator door closes and the elevator begins to rise, you feel the weight of gravity and the surroundings pressing in upon you. But, as you continue ascending, this heaviness leaves and in a few seconds you seem to catch up with the elevator's movement and then begin to rise with it. As the elevator slows for the approaching stop, your sensation is to want to go higher and continue upwards.

So it is with a daily devotional time. It should carry your thoughts onward and upward toward God. It should be a refreshing time, something to look forward to and something to desire. It's the start of a new day and spending a few minutes in prayer, Bible reading, a daily devotional reading and in worship, you will face your new day correctly. Your focus will be on the Lord. That way, no matter what that day brings you, you will be properly outfitted in the "armor of God."

As it says in Ephesians 6:11-16, "Put on the whole armor of God, that you may be able to stand against the wiles of the devil. For we are not contending against flesh and blood, but against the principalities, against the powers, against the world rulers of the present darkness, against the spiritual hosts of wickedness in the heavenly places. Therefore, take the whole armor of God, that you may be able to withstand in the evil day, and having done all, to stand. Stand therefore, having girded your loins with truth, and having put on the breastplate of righteousness, and having shod your feet with the equipment of the gospel of peace; above all taking the shield of faith, with which you can quench all the flaming darts of the evil one. And take the helmet of salvation, and the sword of the Spirit, which is the word of God."

Prayer

Lord, give me the perseverance to begin each of my days in a quiet time of prayer, Bible reading, daily devotional reading and worship. Help me to do this so that, like the old lady's wire basket when filled with water, I will be "a little cleaner" and a little closer to you when my quiet time is finished. Help me, like an airplane or an elevator, to strive upwards towards you in my thoughts and actions and help me to be able to face the events of each day properly outfitted in the whole armor of God, that you will be with me in the midst of all the day's events. Amen

Devotional Reading #2

Fill Your Cup Each Day

Many people can't seem to start their day without a cup of coffee. If they don't have a cup before they leave the house in morning, they certainly have one soon after they arrive at work.

Let's just pretend that this day you do something a little different. Let's pretend that you are being given a handful of pebbles, all different sizes, colors and shapes. Let's pretend that you take your coffee cup and the handful of pebbles and you sit down at a table.

Now, think about what you did upon getting out of bed this morning. Undoubtedly, you may have washed your face, taken a shower or a bath to freshen up and begin your day. Pick out a pebble and put it into your cup. The pebble represents having done that activity. Next, you probably put on your clothes, so put another pebble into your cup. Did you brush your teeth? Put another pebble into your cup. Did you comb your hair? Put on makeup? Eat breakfast? Put more pebbles into your cup.

Thus, proceed...throughout the day, putting pebbles into your cup...each pebble representing an activity you do. The more important events should be represented by larger pebbles, the lesser important events by smaller pebbles.

Undoubtedly, before your day is even half over your cup will be almost full of pebbles. Nevertheless, get as many pebbles into your cup as you are able.

Now, you know that you should make room in your daily life for "a quiet time with the Lord," yet here you have your cup and it is full of pebbles, all representing the things you do in the course of the day. There seems to be no more room. Your cup is filled to overflowing. And, unless you actually did spend a quiet time with the Lord, and thus you're able to put a pebble into your cup, what will happen to your day? What will happen to all these "pebble events" in your day? Well, it's really quite simple. The pebbles will all remain independent of one another and your day will be just a series of individual events filling your day.

But, now go and get a glass of water and pour that water into your cup of pebbles. Fill your cup with as much water as you can. Suddenly, if you move the cup a little, you can see that the pebbles relate to one another differently. They move against each other, back and forth, sliding this way and that way. Yet, there is no friction, no irritation; they seem to glide around, over and under each other.

If you let this water represent God's Spirit, you can see that His Spirit can move freely throughout your cup filling in the empty spaces between the pebbles. By recognizing God's presence in all the things you do each day you can be assured that your cup of life has truly been filled to overflowing!

Prayer:

Oh, Lord, you've given me twenty four hours for each day. What I do with those twenty four hours depends pretty much on my choices. While there are some things that I must do (i.e. work, school, take care of my children, etc.), nevertheless, there are few other people or events who can require use of my hours. The choice is mostly mine. I can cram those hours full of activities or I can do nearly nothing, choosing instead, to take it easy.

Help me, Oh Lord, to do my tasks well and above all...to be IN those tasks WITH me. Be present in my day. Move throughout my day, Oh Lord, and send down your Holy Spirit to guide, direct and protect me, in all that I do. Amen

Devotional Reading #3

God is My Rock and My Fortress

Once in awhile we find ourselves discouraged, disappointed and maybe even depressed. Sometimes our condition seems almost more than we can handle. Maybe there's a reason for it and maybe it's just because once in awhile "our humanness gets the best of us."

Try to picture this: Today, you are feeling this way. You feel sad and unhappy. Things just aren't right with you and because you don't want to burden anyone with your feelings, you slip away, if only in your mind, perhaps mentally, to a mountain stream. There you crawl out onto a big, flat rock that juts out into that stream. It's a nice morning. The sky is blue, the sun is out. It may turn out to be a nice day, weather wise. You sit there with your knees drawn up to your chest. You listen to the sound of the rushing mountain stream as it swirls and tumbles down the mountainside, its destination somewhere below in the valley. You look up at the trees and watch their branches move gently back and forth in the breeze.

It's warm enough for you to take off your shoes and, with your toes, you test out the temperature of the mountain stream. You notice that the rock you're sitting on has multi-colored lichen growing on it and you notice how God has created it in different colors.

Your mind wanders, but eventually it comes to focus on a partially submerged rock in the middle of the stream. As you watch the water tumbling, bubbling, and foaming around that rock you become mesmerized to such a degree that you begin to forget how you feel…your sadness, your depression. Gradually, you begin to identify with that rock. You begin to wonder what it would feel like to BE that rock. In your mind you become that rock and as that rock, you want to stay there and not be dislodged and swept away. The water hits against your sides and you must brace yourself against the force. You hold fast to your spot in the middle of that stream and each time the water hits you, you fight with it. You conquer it, and the next time the water's force hits, you're prepared.

Then, you imagine that the force of the water breaks off small rock pieces. Sharp edges are chipped off. The water is cold wherever it hits a spot that's been chipped off. It's a new sensation for that spot. Nevertheless, as you think about those rough, sharp edges, you realize that they aren't needed. In fact, you're becoming a better, stronger rock because you got rid of those edges. A new rock formation is emerging. There's healing in that spot where there'd been a rough, sharp edge.

Suddenly, as you watch that rock an unexpected amount of water completely engulfs it and you're brought back to reality with a jolt. And, just as suddenly as the rock was engulfed and submerged, it reappears. It's still there, in the same spot in the middle of the stream. You're relieved that it's still there.

But, now you sit back and begin to think about how concentrating on that partially submerged rock in that mountain stream has changed your feelings. You no longer feel as sad or depressed. Somehow everything has changed. You begin to notice that the heavy feeling you had has lifted. There's even a sense of happiness and new found strength within you. Looking about, you realize that even in nature, there are struggles and sometimes they are against terrific odds. Thus, it is in life, but if you face those odds with determination, conviction...and the Lord, Jesus Christ, you'll be successful.

In 2 Samuel 22:2-7, we read: "...The Lord is my rock, and my fortress, and my deliverer, my God, my rock, in whom I take refuge, my shield and the horn of my salvation, my stronghold and my refuge, my savior; thou savest me from violence. I call upon the Lord, who is worthy to be praised, and I am saved from my enemies. For the waves of death encompassed me, the torrents of perdition assailed me; the cords of Sheol entangled me, the snares of death confronted me. In my distress, I called upon the Lord; to my God I called. From his temple he heard my voice, and my cry came to his ears."

And, in 2 Samuel 22:17-20, it says: "He reached from on high, he took me, he drew me out of many waters, He delivered me from my strong enemy, from those who hated me; for they were too mighty for me. They came upon me in the day of my calamity; but the Lord was my stay. He brought forth into a broad place; he delivered me, because he delighted in me."

And, in verse 47: "The Lord lives; and blessed by my rock, and exalted be my God, the rock of my salvation."

Prayer:

Oh, Lord, help me to cling to you as "my rock," my fortress, my deliverer, my rock of salvation. Be my fortress, my stronghold and my refuge. When the waters of discouragement, disappointment and depression cause me to be sad or unhappy, help me to look to you as my source of strength and comfort. Regardless of what comes my way today, help me to remember that you are my rock and my fortress...in all things and in all situations. Amen

Devotional Reading #4

The Spirit Of God

Do you sometimes question the existence of God? Have you ever seen God or heard His voice. Probably not. Do you know of anyone who has seen Him or heard His voice? Maybe, maybe not. But, in the Old Testament, you know that the people of Israel heard the voice of God. Moses was with God when he went up on Mount Sinai where he received the Ten Commandments. Of course, in the New Testament, Jesus heard the voice of God, the Father, shortly after he'd been baptized in the Jordan River by John the Baptist. Matthew 3:17, says: "and lo, a voice from heaven, saying "This is my beloved Son, with whom I am well pleased."

Perhaps you can name others who have seen God or heard His voice. Nevertheless, it's always difficult to understand the concept of "God;" some people think of God and religion as "mind games." Some people go so far as to say that God and religion form a crutch that weak minded people lean on for support. Scientists often have a hard time believing in God because they can't "measure anything" or "perform any test that will prove that there is a God." And, some people just choose not to believe in God. It often seems as though the more we discuss "God", the more complex and confusing the subject becomes.

This is where "faith" comes into the picture. We have to believe what we read in the Bible. We have to believe that God DID create the earth and all that's on the earth. In the first chapter of Genesis it tells how God did this. Beginning with the first verse, it says: "In the beginning God created the heavens and the earth. The earth was without form and void, and darkness was upon the face of the deep; and the Spirit of God was moving over the face of the waters. And God said, "Let there be light"; and there was light. And God saw that the light was good; and God separated the light from the darkness. God called the light Day, and the darkness he called Night. And there was evening and there was morning, one day. And God said, "Let there be a firmament in the midst of the waters, and let it separate the waters from the waters."

Just reading this much of the first Chapter of Genesis we can see that the Spirit of God is VERY powerful and in this case it only had to move OVER the face of the waters to change it.

Imagine doing a little experiment (or you can actually do the experiment) to illustrate the Spirit of God: Imagine getting a glass and filling it full of water. Imagine adding a little vinegar to it. Did the appearance of the water change any? (No, not much.) Next pretend that you place a sheet of plastic wrap tightly over the top of the glass.

Now, this glass of water-vinegar represents you, a human being. The plastic wrap over the top of the glass may represent a protective shield that a lot of people put up around themselves. It protects them from a variety of influences, ideas, dangers, etc., and it prohibits others from getting to know them too well. It's their defense mechanism. It can also represent a barrier that many people put up against God. They don't want Him to come into their lives and disturb them.

Now, notice how calm and still the water is within the glass. Standing on the table, there is no movement of the water. Then, if we shake the glass, the water moves, but quickly returns to its quiet state once we put it back on the table.

Now, however, imagine that you make a small hole (about the size of a dime) in the top of the plastic wrap. Taking some baking soda (which represents the Spirit of God because of its white color), you pour some through the hole in the top of the plastic wrap. Once it hits the water-vinegar, what happens? Can you guess? (Or if you've really performed this little experiment, you can see for yourself what happens.) Can you see that it foams and bubbles up? The more baking soda you allow to enter, the more violent the action of the water. Clearly, a chemical reaction has occurred. The water's been changed by the addition of the vinegar, yes, but only when the baking soda's added do you notice a real change. The more you add, the more reaction, until the whole glass of water is fizzing and bubbling.

So it is with the Spirit of God in our lives. We can't see it as it enters our bodies, but we are forever changed when it does enter; we will never be the same.

Prayer:

I ask you, Spirit of God, through the power of the Holy Spirit, to come into my life. Stir up my faith! Increase my faith! Awaken my faith in areas where I need stirring up! Help me to take off any protective shield that I've placed around myself, that's keeping you from me. Take up residence in me, O Lord, and let your Spirit flow through me, melting me, molding me, and changing me. Amen

Darkness or Light

The Carlsbad Caverns of New Mexico are among the most intriguing creations in the world. All cave trips are impressive, but none can compare with Carlsbad for beauty and size. To describe the size and beauty is all but impossible, but a few facts will give you an idea of their immense size.

The natural opening to the Caverns is approximately one hundred feet across and possibly thirty to sixty feet high. One of the rooms in the Caverns has been used for a lunch room and has accommodated more than 1200 people at one time. Actually, it served 2000 people during a one hour period.

Another room, called the "Big Room" is shaped roughly in the form of a cross. The staff of the cross measures some 2000 feet; the cross arm is slightly over half that length. The ceiling of this room is 285 feet above the floor. It's staggering to visualize a room underground that's a half mile in length and over one-fourth mile in width. A city block is approximately 300 feet, and using this as a yard stick, the Big Room is close to seven blocks long and over three blocks wide. Some of the formations within this room stagger the imagination. The Giant Dome stalagmite is 62 feet high and 16 feet in diameter. Another formation, the Rock of Ages, is almost as large.

When Carlsbad Caverns first opened to the public it was customary for the guide to light a candle upon entering the Big Room and to place it on an elevated rock. Later, the guide told the group that they will be asked to look at the candle once they are at the opposite end of the room.

When the group reached the Rock of Ages stalagmite, the guide turned out all of the lights and the people were asked to look back at the lighted candle. It could hardly be seen it was so small. Then, the candle was snuffed out and total darkness engulfed the room.

After a moment of complete silence, the guide mentioned how fortunate we are to live in America where the light of freedom burns so brightly. He referred to leaders in other countries that forbid freedoms of the people, where people are often tortured or murdered.

As the guide spoke, I thought, also, about the plight of Christians down through the ages. When Caesar and King Herod had tried to put out the spark of the Christian flame. As part of a fledgling religion in its infancy, Christians, though persecuted and tortured, imprisoned or murdered, had defied those who tried to stamp out their religious beliefs. Sometimes, over the ages, Christianity seemed almost smothered and destroyed. But, then there always seemed to be a small flame that continued to burn. And, then sometimes that small flame would burst forth and shine more brilliantly than ever. God, down through the ages, has forbidden the Christian flame to go out!

In the Bible, in Acts 9:1-9, we're reminded of what happened to one leader because he'd persecuted the followers of Jesus. It says: "But Saul, still breathing threats and murder against the disciples of the Lord, went to the high priest, and asked him for letters to the synagogues at Damascus, so that if he found any belonging to the Way, men or women, he might bring them to Jerusalem. Now as he journeyed he approached Damascus, and suddenly a light from heaven flashed about him. And he fell to the ground and heard a voice saying to him, 'Saul, Saul, why do you persecute me?' And he said, 'Who are you, Lord?' And he said 'I am Jesus, whom you are persecuting; but rise and enter the city and you will be told what you are to do.' The men who were traveling with him stood speechless, hearing the voice but seeing no one. Saul arose from the ground; and when his eyes were opened, he could see nothing; so they led him by the hand and brought him into Damascus. And for three days he was without sight, and neither ate nor drank."

Prayer:

Oh, Lord, help me to let the Light that represents you, Jesus Christ, shine brightly in my life. Help me to remember your presence in my life at all times and to always be an credit to the Christian faith. Help me to always behave in such a manner that others will know that I'm one of your followers. Help me to always say words that are wise and kind. Amen

Devotional Reading #6

Let The Lord Direct

Have you ever walked along a rocky beach looking for specially colored stones and seashells? Have you ever lost track of time doing this? Have you ever become so engrossed in your search that you gave no thought to where you were going or where your pathway was headed?

Picture this: It's a day with lazy clouds dotting the blue sky overhead and a gentle breeze off the lake brushes through your hair. Overhead, seagulls swoop and circle about, giving directions on where there's a fish or piece of food for the taking. It's a cool, but pleasant day. You're about 10 or 12 years old and, alone, you're searching for special stones along a rocky beach somewhere. The wonders of the beachfront excite you as... here is a special stone, there is a special stone and each one is picked up, examined and put into your pocket. Sometimes, a snail shell or a seashell is spotted and it, too, is examined and put into your pocket. Your eyes are always searching about, looking this way and that way, always looking for something EXTRA special and unusual, something that would be deemed "a treasure and admired by all who see it". Your pockets are filling up and so you begin using the bottom of your shirt as a "basket," holding the bottom hem with one hand and still picking up keepsakes with your other hand. Your shoes or sandals are filling up with sand and still you trudge onwards, always looking.

Suddenly, you stop dead in your tracks! You freeze! Your eyes are as big as saucers as you stand motionless! There, directly ahead of your next step is a coiled up snake sleeping in the warmth of the sun. Aghast and terrified, you slowly lower your foot and carefully back away as quietly as possible, hoping against hope that you won't awaken that snake!

In Proverbs 16:9, we read, "A man's mind plans his way, but the Lord directs his steps." And, in Proverbs 20:24, we read, "A man's steps are ordered by the Lord."

Today, I received an e-mail on my computer that further illustrates these Bible verses. The story goes like this: A young man who had been raised as an atheist was training to be an Olympic diver. The only religious influence in his life came from his outspoken Christian friend. The young diver never really paid much attention to his friend's sermons, but he heard them often.

One night the diver went to the indoor pool at the college he attended. The lights were all off, but as the pool had big skylights and the moon was bright, there was light to practice by.

The young man climbed up to the highest diving board and as he turned his back to the pool on the edge of the board and extended his arms out, he saw his shadow on the wall. The shadow of his body was in the shape of a cross. Instead of diving, he knelt down and finally asked God to come into his life.

As the young man stood up, a maintenance man walked in and turned on the lights. The pool had been drained for repairs. (Author unknown)

Thus, it is that the Lord often directs our footsteps and our pathways.

Meditate on these verses found within Psalms 77:13-19, "Thy way, O God, is holy, What god is great like our God? Thou are the God who workest wonders...When the waters saw thee, O God, when the waters saw thee, they were afraid, yea, the deep trembled. The clouds poured out water; the skies gave forth thunder; thy arrows flashed on every side. The crash of thy thunder was in the whirlwind; thy lightnings lighted up the world; the earth trembled and shook. Thy way was through the sea, thy path through the great waters; yet thy footprints were unseen."

"Yet thy footprints were unseen"...yes, not only does the Lord God direct the waters of the earth, but He's directing our footsteps and our pathways in life. Often times we aren't aware that He is at work because his footprints are unseen, but just as a snake was not stepped on in the first story or a diver didn't dive in the second story, the Lord is there directing our footsteps and our pathways.

Prayer:

Oh, Lord, come into my life afresh and anew today. Take charge of my life and direct my footsteps and my pathways. Amen

Follow The Clues And Signposts

Imagine this: You are at summer camp and the camp director has just announced that there will be a treasure hunt. You are told that all campers will be divided into small groups and each group is to compete with the other groups to find the treasure at the end of the hunt. Each group's clues are different and the first group to find the treasure will be rewarded. The treasure will be theirs to enjoy!

The camp counselors help the campers number off by fours... one, two, three, four...and form four groups. Then the camp director gives each group their first clue and you crowd around the person in your group who has that clue. Where does it tell you to go? Which direction? Is it inside a building or outside? How far must you go to find the next clue? What will the treasure be?

Full of questions, heightened anticipation and much excitement, the four groups scatter and the hunt is on!

The clues lead the groups over hills and over dales, under signposts and over lampposts, inside buildings and outside buildings. Some clues are easily found and others take concerted teamwork to figure out and find.

Finally, after many hours in an exhausting afternoon, your group finds the final clue, the one that tells where the treasure is located. The clue says: Go back to camp, go down to the campfire ring on the beach and sit down on the benches, your reward, your treasure, will be given to you! At breakneck speed and on the run, your group goes back to camp and down to the campfire ring on the beach.

And there, within minutes of each other, the other three groups arrive, and the camp director says "Well done...each of you…and now…here's your reward!" Suddenly, with a bang, the campfire erupts into a flaming bonfire and all the camp counselor's come running from the mess hall, each carrying part of your reward…hot dogs, pizza, hamburgers, sloppy joes, potato salad, baked beans, potato chips, jello cups, koolaid and cans of pop, plus cake and ice cream. What a feast! What a reward! All the things you like to eat!

The Lord God Almighty gave each of us clues as to how he wants us to live life. Beginning with the Ten Commandments in the Old Testament and continuing on into the New Testament, there are clues and signposts as to how we are to live. The Ten Commandments (Exodus 19-20) state that (1) You shall worship no other God but me, (2) You shall not make any statue or picture to worship, (3) You shall not speak the name of the Lord except with reverence, (4) You shall keep the sabbath, the seventh day, as a holy day of rest, for in six days I made the world, but on the seventh day I rested, (5) You shall show respect to your father and mother, (6) You shall not commit murder, (7) You shall not be unfaithful to your husband or wife, (8) You shall not steal, (9) You shall not speak falsely against others, (10) You shall not envy another person's possessions.

And, then in the New Testament when Jesus Christ spoke to the crowds who'd gathered on the mountainside, he said: "Blessed are the gentle, for they shall inherit the earth. Blessed are the merciful, for they shall be shown mercy. Blessed are the pure in heart, for they shall see God. Blessed are the peacemakers, for they shall be called the children of God. Blessed are those who are humble, those who are just, those who try to do right, those who suffer persecution - all of them will be rewarded in the kingdom of Heaven.

The mountainside where Christ delivered these words is called "The Mount of Beatitudes". It's a low hill near Capernaum and overlooks the Sea of Galilee. The word "beatitude" means "blessed" and refers to the sayings of Jesus that begin with the words "blessed are…" These beatitudes describe the qualities of the ideal follower of Jesus.

In the New Testament there are many clues and signposts that point to the desired behaviors that the followers of Jesus are to exhibit.

In John 14:6, it says, "I am the way, and the truth, and the life; no one comes to the Father, but by me." And, so it is…if we ask Jesus Christ into our life as our personal Lord and Savior, if we confess our sins and repent, if we believe that Jesus died on the cross for our sins and that He rose from the grave, and if we keep ever mindful of all of the clues and signposts that should keep us "on the straight and narrow pathway"…ultimately, we will receive the reward, the treasure. That reward, that treasure is "life eternal." We will spend eternity with the Lord God Almighty!

Prayer:

Oh, Lord, I ask that you forgive me of my sins, voluntary and involuntary, known and unknown. I ask you to come into my life anew and afresh this day. Help me to be ever mindful of the clues and signposts that you've set forth in the Holy Bible that help me to live a life acceptable to you. Help me to work diligently to be acceptable, but to also remember that Jesus was the supreme sacrificial lamb and when he died on the cross he paid the penalty for my sins. Help me this day, oh Lord, to deal with the different clues and signposts that come my way in such a manner that one day, when my life on earth is ended you will say, "Well done, good and faithful servant; you have been faithful over a little, I will set you over much; enter into the joy of your master." (Matthew 25:21) Amen